Structure and Spontaneity:
the process drama of Cecily O'Neill

Structure and Spontaneity:
the process drama of Cecily O'Neill

Philip Taylor and
Christine D. Warner

With a Foreword by Gavin Bolton

Trentham Books

Stoke on Trent, UK and Sterling, USA

Trentham Books Limited
Westview House   22883 Quicksilver Drive
734 London Road   Sterling
Oakhill   VA 20166-2012
Stoke on Trent   USA
Staffordshire
England ST4 5NP

First published 2006

British Library Cataloguing-in-Publication Data
A catalogue record for this book is available from the British Library

ISBN-13: 978 1 85856 322 0
ISBN-10: 1 85856 322 4

The cover image is from a production of Bertolt Brecht's *The Caucasian
Chalk Circle* featuring Daryl Embry, Caitlin Heibach, Christopher Peterson
and Annie Montgomery, directed by Philip Taylor in the Provincetown
Playhouse, New York City, in November 2004.
Photograph by Chianan Yen, used with permission.

Designed and typeset by Trentham Print Design Ltd, Chester
Printed and bound in Great Britain by 4edge Limited, Hockley

Contents

To Gavin Bolton and Dorothy Heathcote

Acknowledgements

This project has been a labour of love. We are indebted to Cecily O'Neill for entrusting us with her papers and for being a constant source of patience and guidance. The editors would like to thank the following publications for permission to reprint material: *Design for the Arts in Education, English Journal, Encyclopaedia of English Studies and Language Arts, Heinemann, IDEA Publications, Language Arts, Captus Press, National Association for Youth Drama, Theatre First, The Journal of National Drama, Theory into Practice* (The Ohio State University), and *Taylor and Francis (Falmer Press)*. We are grateful to Professor Katherine Burkman and Charles Young. Both editors wish to acknowledge the enthusiastic support from their two different institutions: The Ohio State University, College of Education and Human Ecology, as well as New York University, The Steinhardt School. Many thanks to all those who assisted in keying in articles, checking references and securing permissions: from New York University: Amy Cordileone, Kristy Messer, Zachary Moore, Dani Snyder and Brad Vincent; from The Ohio State University: Catherine Hughes. Of special note, *The Recruiting Officer* process drama was ably transcribed by David Montgomery. We thank all those students who participated in this drama through NYU's 2003 summer study abroad program in London. We acknowledge Nancy Swortzell's dedication to co-ordinating this international effort over a thirty year period, and for bringing the best of British innovation in drama education to American and worldwide teachers. Nancy retired from this formative study abroad program – the year of *The Recruiting Officer* but she enabled US educators to work consistently with O'Neill in England since the summer of 1990. The cover image is from a production of Bertolt Brecht's *The Caucasian Chalk Circle* featuring Daryl Embry, Caitlin Heibach, Christopher Peterson and Annie Montgomery, directed by Philip Taylor in the Provincetown Playhouse, New York City, in November 2004. Photograph by Chianan Yen, used with permission. Kudos to Trentham Books and Gillian Klein for building the international drama education list and for accepting this title. Cecily O'Neill is one of the most influential figures in drama education today and we believe this collection will be a timely and integral addition to scholarship. In relatively small disciplines like drama education we are fortunate to have a publishing house that will support important new works.

About the Editors

Philip Taylor, PhD, is Director of New York University's Program in Educational Theatre. Books include *Assessment in Arts Education; The Drama Classroom: Action, Reflection, Transformation; Applied Theatre; Researching Drama and Arts Education, and Redcoats and Patriots: Reflective Practice in Drama and Social Studies.* Taylor was instrumental in establishing the International Drama in Education Research Institute (IDIERI). As an undergraduate in Australia he recalls watching seven minutes of videotape of Dorothy Heathcote working with disaffected youth which made him realise that there were different ways of collaborating in the drama classroom. Ironically, he is currently working on a new prison theatre project in New York State. He has studied with many of the principal leaders in process drama but it was Cecily O'Neill's summer school at OSU, and her process drama on 'The Quest', that enabled him to understand how to structure innovative praxis for spontaneous encounters.

Christine D. Warner, PhD, a former student of Cecily O'Neill, focuses her practice and research on drama in education learning methodologies, interdisciplinary enquiry, cognition and expertise thinking. Prior to her university teaching, Christine taught language arts and theatre in classrooms that were located in a inner-city high school in Washington D.C. and a college preparatory school in El Paso, Texas. Christine continues her teaching practice in both the elementary/ middle school and university classrooms on Native American Reservations in New Mexico and Montana. When Christine is not teaching on the reservation she is an Associate Professor at The Ohio State University in the College of Education and Human Ecology where her focus is teaching drama in education, enquiry and integrated curriculum methodologies to pre-service teachers as well as graduate students. Her work is significantly influenced by Cecily O'Neill and Dorothy Heathcote.

Foreword

I t was in June 1978. The senior external examiner appointed by the University of Durham, in addressing the MA tutors, waved Cecily O'Neill's dissertation at us and declared that in all his examining experience, this was the best dissertation he had ever read. Such comments – indeed, any comments – made at an Examination Board meeting are regarded as confidential, so I have not made this public until now ... (you won't tell anyone will you!)

I am thrilled to discover that at least a section of that dissertation is published, albeit 28 years later, within this volume. Philip and Christine, both so close to her work over many years, have put together a selection of writings by or about Cecily that gives us a glimpse of the many sides to her professional self. We see O'Neill the academic investigating the significance of form in classroom drama. We see her as an artist in the classroom, both leading and following as her classes create. Her skill as an analyser of practice emerges – a critical but constructive observer of both her own teaching and that of others.

It is the image of Cecily O'Neill as innovator of a new approach to teaching Drama that best conveys her professional stature. This important turning point in her career began when, as she taught classes of differing ages in classrooms round the world – often on public view with audiences of teachers and students eagerly absorbing her professional skills – she sought to extend the current drama-in-education methodology into a new genre of theatre: process drama. Practical examples of her using this new approach in various educational contexts are set out and analysed in these pages and, importantly, these are accompanied by a philosophical underpinning that both explains and justifies the experimentation. With meticulous argument she outlines a rationale for the practice of process drama, developing a theory born of that practice.

This book celebrates Cecily O'Neill's contribution to education. We thank Philip Taylor and Christine Warner for presenting it in a way that allows us to enjoy and learn from this outstanding teacher.

Gavin Bolton, May 2006

Prologue

In everything I do I am very much aware of all the practitioners and theorists whose work I lean on, as well as those students and educators who have given me so many opportunities to learn from them. Each of us brings something different to our work in drama, and this difference is determined not just by what we know, but by who we are and where we have come from. Everyone will take a different journey, and encounter a range of obstacles, challenges and supports along the way. My support comes from the people I have worked with, the books I have read, the plays I have encountered and the places I have lived in.

I was lucky that my home town was Dublin, a city where talk and argument are a vital part of life. Dance and, later, drama were part of the delight of growing up – using my imagination, developing a sense of self and enlarging my capacities. Even before I went to University College Dublin to take a degree in English and History, dramatic literature was my favourite reading and being involved in theatre my favourite activity. The plays of Yeats, Synge, Wilde, O'Casey, Behan, Beckett and Shaw provided different perspectives on the Ireland I saw around me. These playwrights transformed and embodied the towering figures of legend and history, as well as the ordinary people of rural and urban Ireland. At University, literary and dramatic criticism gave me new insights into their work. Otherwise, the Dramatic Society took up almost all my time, to the inevitable neglect of my studies, but provided moments of the most intense excitement, delight and learning.

After graduation, I married and went to live in London. School had been such a place of boredom that I had always rejected the notion of becoming a teacher, the obvious profession for someone with an Arts degree and no other professional training. However, in the 1960s London schools were short of teachers, and as a graduate it was possible to get immediate certification. With three small children, teaching seemed the only career I could practically undertake, so I became a teacher of English and, almost by default, a drama teacher.

I first recognised the value of improvisation when I was working in an academic secondary school. I was preparing my students for public examinations, and they were studying Jacobean tragedies – *The Changeling* and *The Duchess of Malfi*. Although I knew very little about improvisational techniques, the immediate difference a few simple activities made to my students' understanding was so impressive that I was determined to pursue this approach. A variety of part-time courses followed: on Brian Way, Peter Slade, Viola Spolin, as well as mime, movement and drama therapy. One of the most impressive teachers I encountered at this time was Keith Johnstone, and his work continues to be an inspiration in its immediacy, inventiveness and artistry. His book, *Impro*, is extremely insightful, not just about improvisation and the theatre, but also about the task of teaching.

In the mid-seventies, I was employed as Warden of the Inner London Education Authority's Drama and Tape Centre, with responsibility for delivering in-service courses in drama with my colleagues, the drama advisory teachers. We were supposed to be experts, but I was only too aware of great gaps in my knowledge and experience. Together we struggled to make sense of drama for the teachers who attended our courses, and the result was *Drama Guidelines*, a handbook that beginners in the field found useful, perhaps because of its simplicity.

At this time, I encountered the work of Dorothy Heathcote and Gavin Bolton. Their understanding of the power of drama as a medium for learning as well as an art form was enormously influential. I took a year's sabbatical and did an MA degree with Gavin Bolton at Durham University. He was working on *Towards a Theory of Drama in Education*, and his analysis of different modes of drama and the structuring of episodes within the process provided real enlightenment. I took every opportunity to observe Heathcote's work with students and teachers at Newcastle University.

I have learned almost everything I know about drama from these two outstanding theorists and practitioners, and from the dramatic literature which first drew me to the subject. *Drama Structures*, written with my colleague Alan Lambert, was an attempt to clarify some of what we had learned from Bolton and Heathcote, and to make their methods accessible to other teachers. *Dorothy Heathcote: Collected Writings on Education and Drama*, co-edited with Liz Johnson, provided a wonderful opportunity to encounter and make more widely available Heathcote's profoundly influential ideas on teaching and drama and the dynamic relationship between them.

My studies at Durham led to an interest in the theoretical foundations of drama in education, and especially in aesthetics. It was a struggle for me to connect what I knew of dramatic form with my growing understanding of the way in which drama in education operated. I was captivated by the work of Suzanne Langer and John Dewey, among others, and began to read as much as possible about dramatic theory. The work of American critics, like Bert States and Richard Hornby, as well as those more involved in performance such as Richard Schechner and Robert Foreman, continues to be illuminating.

In 1987 I accepted a position at The Ohio State University, where I had responsibility for drama and theatre education within the College of Education. This position gave me the opportunity to work with PhD and MA students and to certify teachers in Drama and Theatre. In the States such positions are more likely to occur in Theatre Departments, and often focus more on Children's Theatre and Creative Dramatics than on drama in the curriculum. I was fortunate that the work of Dorothy Heathcote was recognised at Ohio State. She had taught there several times in the 1970s and many of the faculty remembered the power of her work and its potential for learning within the curriculum.

Although the American educational tradition has an emphasis on product, there are many fine teachers and teacher educators in Ohio and elsewhere in the States who have put drama in education at the heart of their curriculum. *Dreamseekers: Creative Approaches to the African American Heritage*, edited with Anita Manley, is a record of their inspirational work.

I am now based in London with my husband Colm, whom I met at university in Dublin. He has always supported and encouraged me, as have our children, Rachel, Hugh and Dan, who share our involvement in theatre. My grandchildren Alex, William, Ronan and Maya all help me to keep the spirit of play alive in my life[1].

Since leaving OSU in 1999, I have had the opportunity to travel widely, lecturing and giving workshops in schools, universities and theatres, but I try to find time to work with children in the classroom, which is where my interest in drama in education began. The struggle to make a bridge between our philosophy and practice and the craft and heritage of theatre continues to absorb me. I believe that the power of drama to help students learn about the inner rules of drama through the process of drama has never been fully recognised. Drama in education has the capacity to expose the key dramatic structures and characteristics that it shares with other kinds of theatre, and this is the subject of *Drama Worlds: A Framework for Process Drama*. Students and teachers in many different countries continue to teach me about the power and potential of drama in education, this ephemeral and unpredictable process which is intrinsically dramatic, truly educational, and profoundly worthwhile.

Cecily O'Neill

Note

1 At the time of publication Colm O'Neill passed away following a prolonged illness. Colm was a generous and gentle man who will be greatly missed.

Introduction

So you are interested in process drama and want to understand more about how to design, implement and evaluate a session with integrity and which conforms to dramatic conventions and styles. Where do you begin? It is perhaps overwhelming for beginning drama educators to position themselves within the myriad of texts, pioneers and personalities, to understand the different movements and trends, and to figure out what good drama teaching entails. The field of drama education has had an impressive tradition and for newcomers it can be quite a challenge as they begin to forge their own teaching identity.

In our view, teachers learn best from other teachers, and when they can apply and adapt exemplary models of teaching praxis in their own work. This book is about one teacher, Cecily O'Neill, and her contribution to the field of drama education. It is a text which is not meant to deify O'Neill, but rather to examine and illuminate the characteristics of her praxis as she structured, implemented and reflected upon educational drama. Readers will not need to have any prior understanding of O'Neill's praxis as they read this book. We will be introducing you to the major features of her teaching and demonstrating how influential and helpful these features have been to a range of educators worldwide. When we use the term *praxis* we are referring to a dynamic interplay between theory and practice, where the drama leader is not merely implementing a predetermined sequence of activities but is constantly re-thinking ideas as participants experience the structure. Praxis implies a critical consciousness powered by a desire to heighten reflective and trans-formative educational events.

Why the title, *Structure and Spontaneity?* These are two of the key principles that informed O'Neill's pedagogical approach. In a sense structure and spontaneity are inextricably linked, and they need to be firmly understood if satisfying arts experiences are to be realised. Structure refers to the embedded elements that comprise a teaching-learning encounter. These elements are informed by an artful selection of various strategies and activities that aim to explore an issue, theme or relationship. A session's structure is not a random and isolated sequence of steps. Structure refers to the interrelationship of dramatic episodes, and the manner in which these episodes are composed and articulated. In O'Neill's influential text, *Drama Structures* (1982), which she co authored with Alan Lambert, she argued that careful and coherent structural planning was often missing from a drama curriculum:

> We feel that what is lacking is not access to drama 'ideas', which are provided in many different handbooks, but suggestions for the kinds of structure which will help teachers in extending these ideas and in working in greater depth with their pupils. If pupils are to grasp concepts, understand complex issues, solve problems and work creatively and co-operatively in drama, they will be helped by a clearly established context and a strong but flexible framework to support and extend the meaning of the work. (p9)

Educators might usefully see themselves as structure operators, as they experiment with different strategies and find creative ways of locating them in the drama session. If educators are to have a firm sense of dramatic structure, they need to understand theatrical traditions and genres and they should have a grasp of theatreform and dramaturgy. It is important that educators understand the various movements and philosophies that power a theatrical encounter. Knowledge of naturalism, realism, the epic theatre, agit prop and surrealism, theatre of the absurd, the poor theatre and theatre of the oppressed will inform how teachers design their work. Understanding historical traditions, indigenous and world theatre, the Greeks and Shakespeare, the avant-garde, the dramaturgy of Beckett and Deavere Smith, will shape the structure. In O'Neill's view, innovative learning experiences need to be informed by thoughtful study and rich encounters with theatre in a variety of settings.

> It should be possible to set up a dramatic curriculum for prospective teachers that explores the making of meaning in theatre by a true balance between creation, performance, appraisal, and contextual knowledge and that presents those aspects in an active and dialogic way. It will be important to recognise, above all, that K-12 theatre teachers need to be able to motivate and engage students of different ages in an active relationship with theatre practices, forms and knowledge. This means that the focus of their own training must be on the processes by which theatre comes into being and on the ways in which a context of true dialogue can be created in the classroom. (O'Neill, 1991: 25)

The kind of freedom or spontaneity that often characterises drama encounters will demand that drama teachers can step off the plan and devise work in process. Such requires the ability to collaborate and to read what sense participants are making of the drama structure and how they would like it to unfold. Too often a drama class begins with the all familiar warm-up, followed by an improvisation or some other random activity, culminating with small groups sharing their presentations for the whole class. Often there is no logical connection between the session's components, and teachers seem to be leading students through a set of unrelated tasks with little rhyme or reason. O'Neill is arguing for an enhanced role of the teacher who negotiates a community partnership where all stakeholders have an investment in the quality and themes of the work. This pedagogical approach is now referred to as *process drama*.

> Process drama is almost synonymous with the term drama in education. The phrase process drama seems to have arisen almost simultaneously in Australia and North America in the late 1980s as an attempt to distinguish this particular dramatic approach from less complex and ambitious improvised activities and to locate it in a wider dramatic and theatrical context ... The practices of drama in education and, by extension process drama, are increasingly recognised as radical and coherent theatrical experiences. They challenge traditional notions of the creation and function of character and narrative, as well as of a traditional spectator-performer relationship. In what is one of the first uses of this term in print, Brad Haseman notes that those working in process drama have created, appropriated, and reshaped a range of dramatic forms that establish its unique character. For Haseman, these forms include role taking and role building, the 'key strategy' of teacher-in-role, the means of being inside and outside the action, and distance and reflection. (O'Neill, 1995, xv, xvii-xviii)

While it is understandable that readers might be baffled by the term process drama, arguing that all classroom drama involves process, it is important to know that the term identifies a particular way of working. While process drama shares some of the characteristics of other movements such as the child drama created by Peter Slade, the development through drama advocated by Brian Way and the creative dramatics of Winifred Ward, it is important to appreciate that the term process drama identifies a specific mode of educational praxis (see Chapter One for a further discussion of these movements). Process drama has become one of the more evocative means for educators to construct significant aesthetic events in various educational and community contexts.

The evolution of process drama, the genre of activity rather than the term, is attributed to the innovator Dorothy Heathcote, who in the early 1950s developed a unique and probing approach to drama education (Bolton, 2003). Heathcote's influence on O'Neill's praxis is apparent throughout this text. In the early phases of her career Heathcote advocated that students live through experiences at life's rate. She likened this approach to students being caught up in tension-driven 'messy' situations where they endeavoured to resolve a challenge they were facing. This challenge might involve dealing with betrayal from a supposed ally, journeying to a new land and experiencing hardship, or having to document the fragmentary history of indigenous peoples.

Heathcote grounded her early teaching in the practice of theatre innovators and reminded educators that drama was always contextual, richly layered with resonant meanings. 'Heathcote insists,' writes O'Neill (in Taylor, 1998), 'that in devising fruitful encounters between teacher, students, ideas, knowledge and skills, it is essential to become process-oriented.' This commitment to process places specific demands on educators as they negotiate outcomes with their students and as they endeavour to become authentic. Authenticity in drama teaching requires that educators:

- Learn to present problems uniquely to students
- Discover more subtle forms of induction and communication
- Encourage student interaction and decision making
- Imagine and carry into action a greater variety of tasks
- Develop a range of feedback techniques
- Take risks with materials
- Tolerate ambiguity
- Pay attention (Taylor, 1998, pvi)

While it was Heathcote who provided the initial challenge for teachers to reflect more closely on their evolving aesthetic sensibility, it was Bolton (1979) who pushed O'Neill to develop a theoretical framework. Being an in-service provider to London's teachers, O'Neill was determined to find a way of making complex and sometimes mystifying Heathcotean praxis readily accessible to teachers.

> O'Neill, influenced by (Bolton), developed her own form of process drama. This focused more on theatre form and related less to the deep 'being' in the situation in which Bolton had a life-long interest, although O'Neill was still concerned to find episodes of this at the centre of her work. (Davis, 2005: 174)

Bolton writes in this book (Chapter Two) how O'Neill's praxis evolved over the years, from drama for learning, to drama as art. Ironically, Heathcote's interest moved to the other side of the continuum as she became interested in her mantle of the expert approach. 'Heathcote left behind as a central concern the development of the art form of drama in education,' writes Davis, 'and concerned herself with pedagogy.' (p176) What is being argued here is that the practice of Bolton, Heathcote and O'Neill was transformed over the period of their professional careers.

However, this book is about the process drama of Cecily O'Neill, and how it can be structured to release participants into satisfying and spontaneous experiences. While there are anthologies of the scholarship of Bolton (Davis and Lawrence, 1986) and Heathcote, (Johnson and O'Neill, 1984) there is no collection of O'Neill's formative writings.

Process Drama and Pre-Text

In order to help readers gain a sense of the O'Neill working style, we begin by deconstructing a session which she led with American graduate students in London. These students, a combination of full-time teachers, teaching artists and novices in drama education, were enrolled in a three-week intensive program which aimed to develop their understanding of process drama, and teach them how to structure richly aesthetic classroom events. The students were aware of O'Neill's formative texts *Drama Worlds* (1995) and *Drama Structures* (1982). For many, this was the first time they had experienced an improvised drama since their undergraduate years; their professional lives were now ruled by their ability to lead. O'Neill and the group seemed to share a common understanding. They knew, for instance, that a public performance was not the goal. This workshop was pitched at drama leaders wanting to become more adept at structuring process drama and facilitating sound improvisation. They recognised the allure of negotiated drama as a vehicle for helping children articulate their own special relationship to the world.

The terms process drama and pre-text are ones O'Neill finds useful when characterising the nature and launching strategy of non-scripted collaborative enactment. The participants accepted the following working definitions.

The features of process drama include:
- Separate scenic units linked in an organic manner
- Thematic exploration rather than an isolated or random skit or sketch

- A happening and an experience which does not depend on a written script
- A concern with participants' change in outlook
- Improvisational activity
- Outcomes not predetermined but discovered in process
- A script generated through action
- The leader actively working both within and outside the drama

Fundamental to O'Neill's understanding of process drama is the central role the teacher plays in weaving the artistic event. Rather than a passive observer of the child's drama, O'Neill is pro-active in structuring the material. This pro-activity does not simply mean that the teacher instructs the group what to do, but rather negotiates and re-negotiates the substance and direction of the drama towards an aesthetic experience.

Teachers in process drama should see themselves as:
- Structure operators who weave the units of action together into an artful experience
- Artists, the teachers, collaborating with their students, the co-artists
- Building a work in process
- Able to release themselves from their lesson plan
- Capable of finding questions to explore rather than providing answers
- Raising possibilities rather than confirming probabilities

The launching strategy in process drama is fundamental to its development. O'Neill (1995: xv) calls this launching strategy a pre-text. A pre-text refers to the 'source or impulse for the drama process ... as well as indicating an excuse – a reason for the work – it also carries the meaning of text that exists before the event.'

A pre-text:
- Rings up the curtain by framing the participants effectively and economically in roles that have a firm association with the potential action
- Suggests clear purposes and tasks
- Has a structural function which may be to set up expectations, establish patterns, imply roles, suggest a setting
- Operates as an animating current

- Sets in motion the weaving of the drama: a text is generated by this process
- Hints at previous events and foreshadows future occurrences
- Can be recalled or repeated
- Is not necessarily a text to be written down
- Will give birth to any number of themes

O'Neill finds it useful to consider how playwrights use dramatic form when devising opening scenes. Shakespeare, for instance, usually sows the seeds of the forthcoming action in the first scene. In *Macbeth*, the three witches neatly set in motion the action of the play by introducing darkness/lightness, winning/losing and right/wrong. *Hamlet*, likewise, introduces the themes of deception, disarray and superstition in the first minutes. Our attention is usually arrested by the questions raised, the possibilities considered, a future suggested. Drama teachers, equally, should look for similar portends or echoes of foreboding when they devise their pre-text. A photograph may be an effective pre-text, as may a gesture, a title, a location, an object or an image, or a classic text which is reborn through the drama.

> Drama teachers are familiar with the notion of a `stimulus` as the source of dramatic activity, but a pre-text is rather different. The term `stimulus` carries a disagreeable suggestion of something purely mechanical, rather than conveying a more appropriate and complex organic implication. A pre-text has a much more precise structural function than merely to propose an idea for dramatic exploration. The purpose of the pre-text is to activate the weaving of the text of the drama, because although the drama may not originate in a text, it always generates a text in action. Like a play in the theatre, the text generated by the process is an outcome, a dramatic product, and may be recalled and to some extent repeated. (O'Neill in Taylor, 2000: 25)

Often drama teachers commence their lesson with a warm-up or ice-breaker. This might involve a physical activity, perhaps a game or movement piece which would not necessarily have any relationship to the activities which follow. A pre-text, on the other hand, contains the germ of action which can lead to any particular course in the drama. It is not an isolated activity but an integral one.

> An effective pre-text or preliminary frame for process drama will carry clearly accessible intentions for the roles it suggests – a will to be read, a task to be undertaken, a decision to be made, a puzzle to be solved, a wrong-doer to be discovered, a haunted house to be explored. A popular pre-text among drama teachers is the following announcement, from *Drama Structures*:

$100
offered to anyone willing
to spend one night in
DARKWOOD HOUSE

> This announcement hints at the past and suggests the future, but within a firm dramatic present. It offers a task and implies roles for the participants. It operates functionally in a similar if a much less complex way to Marcellus' question at the beginning of *Hamlet*: 'What, has this thing appeared again tonight?' Here, Shakespeare economically informs us in a single line that it is night time, that a 'thing' has appeared on a previous occasion, and that the characters fully expect it to show up again. (O'Neill, 1995: 20-21)

What follows now is a comprehensive description and analysis of a process drama led by O'Neill. Contained within this analysis are the words of the participants, O'Neill's observations, reflections of other theorists, and a linking commentary. This process drama could be analysed in many ways. The chart below lists O'Neill's suggestions which readers might adopt when organising their responses to process drama.

When analysing process drama the following organising themes or categories may be useful:

- The pre-text and how it articulates with the dramatic action
- Episodes or scenic units and the organic links between them
- Notions of participation and audience
- Engagement (suspending disbelief) and detachment (suspending belief)
- Dramatic irony
- Private and public dimensions
- Particulars and universals
- Emergent themes
- Archetypal elements
- Overlapping worlds, i.e. world of pre-text, of the drama, of the participants

In the following description, it is the first category, i.e. how the pre-text relates to process drama and aspects of the work's artistry, which will be a focus. Readers might later consider the work through other categories listed above or, alternatively, create their own. The boxed sections following the tasks indicate our analysis of the pedagogical-aesthetic principles informing the process drama.

8

The Recruiting Officer: A Process Drama on War and its Aftermath

> My purpose was to develop an extended piece of practical work in drama at the participants' own level, in order to provide material for reflection on the nature of the process. I believe that process drama can be a significant vehicle for prolonged and satisfying experimental encounters with the dramatic medium. Although the extended and essentially improvisatory event that is beginning to be known as process drama will proceed without a pre-written script, an original text is generated in action. The resulting experience for the participants can possess the same coherence, complexity and singularity of any satisfying event. Process drama, while remaining apparently formless and undefined by a previous plan or script, has a special capacity to lay bare the basic dramatic structures that give it life, which it shares with other kinds of theatre. (Cecily O'Neill)

After the group initially canvasses topics for a process drama on such subjects as civil rights, prostitution, racism and the American revolution, it is agreed that the focus will be war. O'Neill decides to assume a role that will unite the group while trading on their feelings of ambiguity and uncertainty.

■ Episode One: Launching the Pre-text

> Task: Teacher assumes the role of a recruiting officer entering a small township

O'Neill (in role as the Recruiting Officer):

> I seldom get to meet such a wonderful group of young people. And I'm here today to offer you an unrivalled opportunity. I know times have been hard here. Real hard. I know there's not much employment. I know some of your families are in want. But because of what I can offer you here today, this is the beginning of a whole new future for you. We need volunteers. And if you agree to join our forces, there are so many ways your life will change. First of all, I don't want to say anything against your town. It's a nice little town. But I have to tell you... I know most of you probably haven't been beyond the boundaries of this town. Let me tell you, at the end of the railway tracks, there's a whole world out there. And you'll get to do so much. You'll get to meet lots of other young people...you'll be trained... there will be travel. You can see the world. I'm sure that many of you, I hope maybe even all of you, will agree to come forward and sign. I don't know if any of you have any questions. I'm sure that you probably saw the posters we put up. But ... maybe some of you do have some questions.

The participants are seated on chairs while O'Neill stands and assumes the role of the recruiting officer. The narrative that O'Neill provides is spontaneous but readers will note there are structured lures. The narrative is characterised by its brevity and lack of illuminating detail. This officer appears quite charming and knowledgeable, but there appears to be a subtext. This pre-text invites numerous questions from the group:

What are the chances that we will see combat?

If you don't get enough recruits are you going to start the draft?

How long are we required to sign up for?

If we don't want combat are there other options?

What should happen if someone wants to leave and go home?

Will my family be compensated if I am killed?

What skills will we be trained in?

Who is the enemy?

With each question O'Neill's intention is to raise mystery in order to elevate the participants' relationship to the work. She does not want to provide too much information but she does establish that there is an enemy who does not share the same values as the township. The drama is about beckoning futures. There is a whole world that lies outside the little town and its inhabitants, unknowingly, are about to have their lives changed forever.

*O'Neill's drama praxis is characterised by **an ability to select a pre-text which contains the seeds of enquiry**.* In this instance, the pre-text is the beguiling recruiting officer who establishes an imaginary township which is isolated and vulnerable, and faces an unknown enemy.

One of Cecily's outstanding characteristics is her economy as a drama teacher. She is a living example of Dorothy Heathcote's maxim, 'less is more', when working in drama. When questioned at her skill at being able to move a class so quickly and intangibly into the implications of a drama situation Cecily's answer was, in point of fact, quite mundane. The question seemed to surprise her, and she was even more surprised when asked about warm ups prior to teaching drama. 'In the kind of job I do,' she said, 'there's no time for anything else but the drama lesson.' (Burke, 1983: 11)

■ Episode Two: Creating the Town

Teacher Narration:

> Once upon a time there was a small town that was experiencing difficulties. This was in the mid-twentieth century. The first half of the twentieth century. And times were very hard. This was partly a farming community but there had been some industry there. By the time our story begins, that was no longer possible. Not many people had jobs. Some families were involved. Young people after they had left school had very few opportunities. Some of them left to go to other cities but many of them stayed and tried to help out – and tried to make a living somehow or other. One day posters were seen around town, shortly followed by a recruiting officer...who explained the advantages of signing up. Of enlisting – and that's the point at which our story begins.

Task: The group is divided into small groups. Half the groups create images of happy memories of life in the town. The other half demonstrate painful memories.

As the groups work to construct an image or tableau which satisfies all members, O'Neill notes the themes which are emerging for this group. There are the happy memories of a town celebrating its history with monument unveilings and award presentations. These are juxtaposed with images of destruction and hardship. The town had experienced brutal bush fires and drought.

As the tableaux are shared, O'Neill is concerned with helping the spectators raise questions which will open enquiry. 'It's not always wise to prioritise the narrative,' she suggests, 'because this fixation on the linear sequence stops the meaning from resonating.' She reminds the group to look at the values and beliefs which the images reveal, rather than guessing what the pictures are actually showing.

The tableau strategy, she reminds the group, is one of the most economical ways of revealing context. Tableaux challenge the participants to watch and respond. Tableaux can help students struggle with ambiguity and deal with multi-faceted readings.

The participants agree with O'Neill when she explains that a frustrating thing for students can be to deal with contradictions. 'How do we help students accept different interpretations of the same event? How can we assist students to tolerate and celebrate difference?'

She deliberately chooses a strategy, in this instance the tableau, which will force divergent thinking. She invites the group to reveal contrasting images, happy and painful memories, as she knows that tension in drama stems from fractured narratives.

O'Neill's praxis is governed by **raising possibilities rather than confirming probabilities**.

> It is not always possible merely to accept and use the pre-text as it stands. Any complex or elaborate pre-text, for example a myth, story or classic text, must be transformed or re-born in the drama. However, powerful traces of the original will resonate in the patterns and relationships that develop during the process. Significant dramatic experiences will not necessarily arise from simply adapting and dramatising what appear to be appropriate pre-texts. This approach is likely to lead to work that is explanatory rather than exploratory, where the ideas and themes are demonstrated and displayed rather than being discovered and explored. Ideally, the pre-text will be sufficiently distorted or reworked so as to be in effect made afresh or transformed. (Cecily O'Neill)

John Dewey (1934) reminds us that in the first phase of the art-making process there is the release of an impulse, an animation towards form or a compulsion to symbolise. In many respects, the telling of the tale in Episode One provides this catalyst for symbolisation. But in process drama it is the move towards physicalising that impulse which triggers the participants to shape their private image into public display. The tableau is an ideal ploy in this initial stage of playmaking. It does not commit the participants to a particular interpretation but rather offers the possibility of multiple interpretations.

■ Episode Three: The family responds to the recruiting officer

Task: Family members who are interested in being recruited inform their loved ones of their desire to go to war.

In small groups, improvisations occur which announce the news that a loved one is attracted to the recruiting officer's invitation. O'Neill challenges the participants to structure work which demonstrates how this news is received in the home. There are diverse responses, from shock that a loved one would be remotely interested in a potentially perilous expedition, to pride in the family member's courage. As the groups share their work, O'Neill is concerned that the audience looks closely at the implications each response has on the family unit. She seeks a range of strategies through which the spectators can be supported in their looking. Sometimes, she invites the thoughts of the participants, occasionally, she provides her own observations.

'The function of this improvisation,' O'Neill reminds the group, 'is for the recruitee, if there's such a word, to begin to see what the reactions of family members might be. And for the rest of us to learn a little bit more about this town and the world in which we live.'

*The teacher structures a moment which supports the experience of those who display and those who watch the display. Again, there is an emphasis on **helping people attend to the moment so that it can be re-born and will fertilise within them.***

A feature of this way of working is the demands that are placed on participants to articulate what they see and never be completely satisfied with the certainty of their observation. In this respect, O'Neill echoes the concerns of the eminent American arts philosopher, Maxine Greene (1994). It is never enough to attend to an art work as something out there that has been defined by official others to be perceived, read or heard as those others decide. The works at hand, Greene contemplates, should become 'objects of experience' for those who come to them.

Such requires an energy, a reaching out, and a care, even a solicitude in noticing, in paying heed to nuance and to detail, and then ordering the parts perceived into a whole within experience. We as teachers are obligated to enable our students to attend well, to pay heed, to notice what might not be noticed in a careless reading or inattentive watching. (p3)

13

Spaces need to be created for students' meaning-making, for their inter-pretations and struggles, which are bound to be numerous. In process drama, strategies are structured which facilitate and empower students to attend to the work and create multiple meanings.

■ Episode Four: The New Recruits Meet the Old Recruits

Entering the war zone occurs through two tasks:

Task One: Photographs of the families are taken on the day the loved one leaves the railway station to go to the war. These are shared with the class.

Task Two: The new recruits (half of the class) arrive at the battle zone. They are immediately thrown into battle, and O'Neill sculpts a narrative which helps establish the context: *'Well it wasn't long before the tensions escalated. The young recruits found themselves in a very rapid training sequence where they were taught just the very basics. And then they were launched into combat far sooner than they had expected. And because of the terrain, and because of the nature of the battle that was going on, it was not the sort of war that they had envisaged. The young recruits found them-selves caught up in small-scale offensives. Most of the terrain was entirely unfamiliar to them because they came from a small farming community. Now they're in among mountains, among forest areas, and they're having to engage the enemy at odd times unexpectedly. Their opponents, their enemies, seem to be committed to fighting with guerilla tactics. And these young recruits are not, as I say, very well trained.'*

The recruits are given a twenty-four hour leave when they meet others who have just arrived. They improvise the encounter which occurs between the old and the new.

Initially O'Neill was not satisfied with how the improvised encounter initially unfolded. There were jubilant exchanges between the old and the new recruits. 'We are not at a high school reunion,' she exclaimed, and then asked the students to repeat the activity. 'You have been in the field for nearly a year. And you have seen things and done things that have made you now not the person you were when you left. Suddenly comes a living reminder of all that. And I don't know to what extent you want to be reminded. I don't know what experiences you may be ready to share. You may be asked about your training. You may be asked about what it's like to be in combat. You may be asked about a lot of stuff, and I don't know how ready you're going to be to share that information.'

O'Neill is reminding the group that they need to be able to read the logic of the dramatic form. The spontaneous responses of the participants required carefully structuring, and O'Neill was endeavouring to elevate the group's ability to create a theatrical canvas.

The teacher develops a community of theatre artists, a community which both controls and is controlled by the form.

Greene reminds us that community cannot be produced through rational formulation or by edict. Like freedom, it has to be 'achieved by persons offered a space in which to discover what they recognise together' and appreciate in common. Wright (in Taylor, 2000: 31) concurs, 'What unites us is the common experience, the investment of time and energy and our innate desire to 'story,' that is, to make sense of our experience.'

■ Episode Five: Experienced Soldiers Reflect on the New Recruits

Task: O'Neill invites some of the experienced soldiers to sit with her in a circle while the rest of the class becomes an audience. These soldiers tell of their encounters with the new recruits from the previous episode. She then invites the newly arrived soldiers to share their experience of talking with the more experienced recruits.

Task: An old recruit and a new one re-create what occurred in their encounter for the whole group.

O'Neill is concerned here that the group reflects for a moment upon the imaginary world which is unfolding. Sometimes participants need to be reminded of the context of a particular encounter and what attitudes might be demonstrated. In the following exchange, notice that the teacher is not reluctant about sharing her own artistic vision. O'Neill helps establish a dramatic context by working in role, yet heightening the reflective skills of all participants. The students' names are pseudonyms.

O'Neill: I'm sick of seeing the new faces. I know there was a face I recognised, but my goodness me ... I mean, where do they think they're coming to? A church picnic? (*To student Jan*) Did you talk to somebody like that?

Jan: Actually there wasn't so much talking. I mean we were together...

Cecily: They look so lost. I mean, did we look like that a year ago?

15

Nat: They looked very optimistic.

Deb: They looked more scared.

Nat: (*To Deb*) No, they had the eyes wide open.

Jan: Scared.

Kate: They asked a lot of questions.

O'Neill: It's so difficult to know what to say isn't it?

Ray: They have no idea what they're getting into.

O'Neill: Well, we didn't either I suppose.

May: I told them to keep their heads down.

O'Neill: Keep their heads down, yeah.

Deb: I saw this kid I went to High School with who I never talked to before. He was one of the popular guys. And, I think he'll be one of the first ones to go. I think he'll be one of the first ones to get blown away.

O'Neill: Too brave?

Deb: No, he's not too brave. Too ... arrogant.

O'Neill: Well then he'll probably be promoted (*all the participants agree*).

Deb: He just doesn't know what he's in for. He's too pretty to be here.

O'Neill then invites the new arrivals to join her in another circle. As in the previous encounter, she assumes the role of a friendly ally, sympathetic to these recruits' experiences.

O'Neill: I don't know about you but it's not like I expected.

Jennifer: I'm worried

Jane: Yes, I'm worried too. He's getting slimmer and slimmer.

O'Neill: Yeah. Well, from what we had to eat just now I don't think the food's that marvellous is it?

Jim: What was it? This meat thing...

O'Neill: If my mother had put that on the table ... you know ... even in our worst times we had better food than that.

Carol: I thought this was going to be exciting. Everyone looked so depressed and...

O'Neill: And bored! They looked bored. I mean how can you be bored? You're in combat. That doesn't seem right.

Vinnie: And half the time they just wait around. Waiting.

O'Neill: Well we could have done that back home.

Carol: This is not like any of the posters I've seen.

O'Neill: That's the truth.

Jim: It didn't seem like they needed us.

O'Neill: If you put some of those guys on posters, I don't think anyone would sign up would they?

Brad: When was the last time they bathed?

Jennifer: She said they don't have to shower every day I couldn't believe it. I could not believe it.

Carol: I don't understand why the petty officers ... why we get such lousy accommodation. And the generals, they have a pretty nice set up over there.

O'Neill: I didn't expect it to be as good as them. But certainly better than this.

Vinnie: Where are the officers?

O'Neill: I don't know. I don't know.

Carol: They were hanging out drinking the last time I saw. And they sure weren't eating with us.

O'Neill: That's true. Well I couldn't find anything out about what combat was like.

Jane: I am missing home.

Carol: I saw somebody from back home, he wasn't even happy to see me. I mean ... he just stared at me like he didn't even recognise me.

Wanda: What did you guys expect? This is war.

O'Neill: It seems more like hanging about to me.

Carol: I didn't expect this. This is not what I signed up for. This is not what the recruiter told me it was going to be like.

The participants now move from playing the roles of the soldiers to reflecting on the nature of the soldiers' experience itself, they project both into and out of the situation. Artistry here is concerned with not locking the participants into one role for too long. O'Neill is suspicious of the kind of drama teaching which demands that students identify with the life of a character for a sustained period of time. She is interested in having participants 'project into the situation in its entirety.' This projection requires participants having access to multiple roles and viewpoints.

O'Neill's attention is arrested by the dramatic action, the behaviour that people adopt within it and the consequent responsibilities and demands

---

which then ensue. Distance from the work is important to developing such projection. 'Engagement in process drama offers participants the opportunity to explore and realise a range of values and identities, and experiment with alternate versions of humanity.' She wants students to develop their own reading of an event which could be compounded if an individual is trapped into one role for any period of time.

Leaders' responses and decision-making in similar episodes have been subjected to considerable criticism from sceptics of process drama. What function does the teacher have? When should teachers assert their own reading of a classroom event? To what extent should teachers layer into the work their own expectations? How do teachers know which risks to take?

A feature of O'Neill's artistry is that she not only construes herself as a co-conspirator with the students but is also sensitive to her own role as leader of an educational experience. Like a painter she manipulates the canvass with her brush, introducing elements which may not have been predicted. The evolving piece gradually suggests possibilities to the artist. At the same time, these possibilities are informed by O'Neill's understanding of what process drama is and what it is not. She knows, for example, that she is not training actors for an academy, i.e. the students are not building skills of characterisation for theatrical performance.

Her drama praxis does not culminate in one aesthetic product which can be assessed and applauded but is driven by an aesthetic process with numerous products to be scrutinised for what they teach. 'It is the responsibility of the teacher or leader,' she says, 'to find a focus that creates an imperative tension and provides a vehicle for the themes and images to be explored.'

The artist releases the participants from the burden of characterisation and presses into the work multiple role perspectives.

■ Episode Six: The Recruits Push On and Ambush a Village

Task: As the old and new recruits move forward, casualties are experienced and some are not able to proceed. The soldiers eventually find themselves behind enemy lines and come to a village. Groups of three demonstrate what happens in the village. 'Just a moment. It doesn't have to be a whole event,' says O'Neill. 'It's like just like an image you would get in your mind.

Like the image of the bunker with the people inside. It can be a good or negative image. It might be an image of heroism. It might be an image of having to save someone. It might be an image of attack. It might be an image of death.'

Task: The villagers from the images are separated from the group. The soldiers take responsibility for one of the villagers. O'Neill reminds the soldiers that the villagers are the enemy and may have vital information they wish to hide. Likewise, she identifies what information the soldiers might want to solicit from those captured. An improvisation occurs between the soldier and the villager. 'Let's see whether at any point humanity emerges between captor and captive,' suggests O'Neill. 'Don't push for it if it doesn't come. But if it comes, think of what triggers it. In a way the improvisation is in the hands of the captives because they're lower status, but also they can call on emotions that the soldier may be having to conceal.' While these improvisations occur, O'Neill moves around the room, in role as a senior officer, engaging with the villagers and soldiers.

Task: The participants reflect on the improvisation. She asks what decisions the soldiers might be faced with now. Concerns about having to feed the prisoners are expressed, as are feelings that some villagers have crucial strategic information which they are hiding. One soldier has thoughts of raping a villager; others express sympathy for the captives.

Here, we begin to see the multi-layered sub-texts that shape the dramatic encounter. Like Heathcote and Bolton, O'Neill does not want participants to jump too quickly into stereotypes, in this instance, of how soldiers and captors might behave. She pushes them to understand the complexity of human endeavour.

> Drama does not exist except when it is occurring; it takes place in a perpetual present tense. Yet this present moment will only have meaning if it carries with it a sense of the past, and is oriented towards the future. Drama does not deal with finished realities or events, as narrative does, but is concerned with future commitments and consequences ... Dorothy Heathcote sums up the idea of time as it operates through the cycle of experience in the drama process in the memorable phrase: 'I rest in the past, I forge the present, I foreshadow the future.' So we may expect experiences in drama, if they are to have significance, to record and sum up the value of what has gone before, and evoke and prophesy what is to come. (O'Neill, 1979: 25)

The juxtaposition of the public world with the private one is a feature of O'Neill's artistic praxis. We have seen in the above episode how both soldiers and captors have hidden intentions which they are not able to reveal. Drama operates on this tension between the presentation and realisation of self. O'Neill finds the work satisfying when there are sub-texts, such as the villagers knowing but not revealing vital information.

Shakespeare's plays richly capture this tension. In *Macbeth*, for example, Lady Macbeth summons up the spirits of evil to represent the incarnation of the devil as she carries out King Duncan's assassination. 'Look like the inno-cent flower,' she cries to her husband on the eve of the murder, 'but be the serpent underneath.' When Duncan arrives at their home with the words, 'This castle hath a pleasant seat; the air/Nimbly and sweetly recommends itself/Unto our gentle senses,' he says one of the classic lines of dramatic irony. Process drama, O'Neill believes, can exploit equally these tensions be-tween public expectation and private knowing.

Drama Praxis is informed by a rich understanding of the artform.

■ Episode Seven: Stakes are Raised

This episode heightens the tension appreciably. Prisoners who are believed to hold information are found accountable and potential punishments are threatened.

Task: Soldiers identify which villagers are suspected of having vital infor-mation concerning the enemy's leadership. Four villagers stand.

Task: Teacher-in-role (O'Neill assumes a senior officer and addresses the following to the villagers). 'You may have heard that we're barbaric. You may have heard that we keep to the words of the war. We tried to do our part. We're trying to get out of this damn village in one piece. And we don't know which of you has information you can tell us, and we don't know which of you is innocent. My soldiers seem to think the majority of prisoners are innocent but that you (pointing to those standing) have information. I would advise you if you know the whereabouts of the leader to tell us now.' The prisoners are pressed to give information. O'Neill tells a soldier to take one of the seated villagers outside and to kill her. Still no information is forthcoming. Other villagers are led out. Some soldiers seem unnerved by this sudden atrocity, others enjoy it.

It is evident that all participants have a stake in the action. In previous episodes the participants have committed themselves to the role of new and experienced recruits, now the plight of the villagers is being demonstrated.

The previous work has prepared the participants to think of themselves as artists shaping content and form. Now the entire group is implicated in taking ownership over their decisions. Soldiers demand that information regarding the whereabouts of the enemy's leadership is revealed. Some villagers are reluctant to name those who are believed to have important information. The stakes are raised as O'Neill assumes a high status role as a senior officer wielding penalties. The episode is fuelled by tension as villagers are escorted to an execution line. Reminiscent of a forum theatre, the participants operate as actor and spectator. This technique is powered by the Brazilian theatre director Augusto Boal's (Cohen-Cruz and Schutzman, 2006) notion of the spect-actor where audience members have an emotional connection to the material. O'Neill often adapts forum theatre into process drama because the spectactors have an ownership in the work's evolution. 'The encounter is being monitored,' she claims, 'and structured by the observers, who, because of their previous involvement, have a considerable investment in it.'

She stops the action at the point where villagers plead for their lives and when some soldiers express concern about the officer's brutal action. The forum theatre is not played through to a culminating point. 'It's about stopping at the moment before it begins to get weaker,' she asserts. Process drama, she repeats, is partly about participants developing the skills to become spectators of their own work and thereby capable of exercising control over it.

'I am in the business of dislocating young minds and am keenly searching for strategies which unsettle, create ambiguity, and force students to struggle with contradictions.' The fact that there is uncertainty challenges the participants to find their own relationship and attitude to the material.

Works of art live through the active engagement and detachment of the viewer with the object. **Fundamental to O'Neill's praxis is the deliberate selection of strategies that pursue engagement and detachment.**

Satisfying encounters with artistic works are often controlled by a participant's desire to engage, an uncompromising wish to be satisfied, and a belief in value and achievement. In this episode, we can see the leader's quest to develop these feelings in her students. Through the process drama, the participants are refining their artistic skills to judge the aptness of a phrase or gesture, to assess the locale and staging, to probe what surprises exist and which moments resonate with indefinable possibilities.

Critics of this mode of working can misjudge the artistic skills that both leaders and their students are clearly cultivating. 'O'Neill,' writes Hughes (in Taylor, 2000) 'is a performance artist who manipulates the drama with the perceptions and skills normally associated with contemporary directors of distinction.' He recalls the manner in which she weaves an aesthetic tapestry which releases the participants to develop their own associations with pre-text.

> Her acknowledgment that the drama teacher is an artist with an agenda precluded the impression, given by so many weak exponents of the art, that the classroom work is somehow no more than a laissez-faire collection of random games and activities. Through O'Neill's structures we (are) enmeshed in a drama net via systematic use of language and action which invite (s) us to engage, respond actively, and oppose or transform enactments ... Her conscious linking of activities to domains as diverse as classical dramatic literature, poetry, folk saga, music, painting, music-theatre and film, indicated that process drama can also illuminate drama as an art-form, an art which presents, represents and reinterprets our social, historical and spiritual consciousness within wider aesthetic spheres. (p37)

To claim, as some have, that process drama denies an interest in artistic products and aesthetic understandings, fails to account for the dynamic interplay between participant and spectator, player and audience, watcher and watched, creator and created: a dialogic relationship which is generated by an unquenchable thirst for understanding; a thirst and venture which is at the centre of all artistic endeavour.

■ Episode Eight: A Universe of Other Texts

Task: The battle escalates between the soldiers and villagers. O'Neill invites the whole group to create one image of the scene of battle.

Task: Students are invited to write a six-line poem from the perspective of a villager or soldier. The first three lines begin with the words 'I was,' the final three with 'I am,' or a combination of both. 'This is a poem,' reminds O'Neill, 'so I don't want you to write... 'I was a farmer once and a soldier'– well, you might begin there, but I want it to be more about what you are on the inside. What you were once, and what you are now as a result of the experiences.' A staged choral reading activity ensues.

The group creates a still image incorporating all participants at the height of the battle. 'And we'll see which of the enemy managed to fight back,' she offers, 'and who will want to change sides and be soldiers.' She invites those who are in the image to step out of it and report back to the group what they see. The observers comment on the terror and the triumph, the bewilderment and the death. There are signs of hope in the utmost decay, the seeds of contrast inform the responses.

As a final reflective activity, the participants are arranged in rows as soldiers and villagers heading toward home. There are three rows: soldiers on the outside, and villagers on the inside. They each select the line from their poem 'I was/I am' that carries the most resonance. O'Neill says that if she had more time she would ask each student to read from another's poem. Such is a further distancing strategy requiring participants to develop yet another perspective on the material.

When the participants read the line from the poem, they move forward as if returning to the place from where they came. 'I want you to walk home, a line at a time,' she says. Reminding the group of their pedagogical as well as their artistic function, she suggests that it is important that the children we teach have their own texts honoured. 'Kids can be keen on their own work but not on another's.' The group is pressed to select words from the writing which evoke the themes explored. 'Only select the words,' O'Neill asserts, 'that are earning their keep and which convey strong images.' The participants stand in choral tradition and create a spontaneous poem. They begin to walk forward and speak. There is a sense of journey and that each has been transported to a different place, changed by their experiences, as the following four lines suggest:

> I was a bird in the winds of change, I am captured in the net of the enemy.
> I was carefree, I am tied to duty.
> I was mother, I am alone.
> I was hopeful, I am hopeless.

While the work culminates in a written poetic text, O'Neill reminds the participants that a number of texts have been generated through the process drama: the teacher's and student's artistic text, the pedagogical text, the director's text, the actor's text, the rehearsal text, the performance text and the audience's text are just some of these. 'Every text,' she recalls, 'lives in a universe of other texts.'

The artist searches for a dramatic form which enables the participants to reveal their relationship to the event.

■ Episode Nine: Deconstructing the War Drama

Task: A discussion occurs on whether the group tackled satisfactorily the topic of war. The group grapples with the question of why educators should structure process drama on this material.

The group begins to clarify the educational and artistic purpose of process drama. At the forefront is the notion of having a satisfying aesthetic experience serving as a basis for group and individual transformation in which participants identify with scenarios, circumstances and human experience. 'This knowing through art can open up new vistas in the life of the senses and of the imagination,' claims O'Neill (1980: 6). 'It can give insight and understanding, although the insight can only exist in the experience, and is in no way translatable. It teaches us to see the world differently.' The great protection for the participants is that they know they are pretending. 'We're not acting at life rate; we are constantly in and out of the experience. We are both soldiers and not soldiers in the war. We are both villagers and not villagers. We have a distance.' This point of view was represented in many of the comments which participants made.

Paul: It got me to think of my role in a situation like this. What questions would come through my head if I was confronted with certain decisions? What would that mean for me personally?

Edie: And going along with that, children are now going through seeing war on television all of the time. Doing this process drama can help them come to an understanding of what war might be like. We get all these TV images thrown at us. Process drama is a way for them to, you know, see how it affects them in a safe environment.

Jane: Kids tend to glorify violence. We need to help them de-glorify it. Process drama is a good way to show them some reality of that.

Lil: Yes, we're asking students to think outside of themselves, to stretch their reality frame.

O'Neill brings closure to the drama by recalling and reminding the group of the journey which inspired their drama and which informed the pre-text.

Drama is good at taking a situation to the extreme. And my favourite quote from the American band, *The Eagles* is, you can 'Take it to the limit one more time.' (*Much laughter.*) In process drama, often you don't just have a fairly bad day— you have a dreadful day! King Lear doesn't just fall out slightly with his daughters— he loses everything. And even when you think it might just turn out good, it doesn't. You can't have a drama about dental hygiene. Well maybe you can, but Shakespeare didn't do it.

For O'Neill, it is the impact of how war changes humanity where artists can most eloquently extend people's frame of reference. 'It's not the battle that's the point,' says O'Neill. 'It's the consequences – it's what war does to people and places.'

We have seen in O'Neill's deliberate structuring of The Recruiting Officer drama, how she is establishing a scaffold where the participants begin to probe their own responses and reaction to a community which is about to be upturned. The participants are both the community and the commentators on the community. While some students might have thought they were in for a bit of a glorious adventure, it was how the teacher layered into the structure lures and challenges which demanded immediate and spontaneous action.

O'Neill does not conclude the process drama with a recognised platitude, a moral certainty or a political correctness. In her mind, such teacher instruction denies the vision and possibility to which artistic works aspire. Aesthetic education requires participants to create their own response based on their particular educational, cultural and ethical context. At the core of this artistic praxis are the elements of reflectiveness, self-discovery and surprise. In process drama diverse ways of being, knowing and art-making can be disclosed. A forever unfinished dialogue is provoked by process drama. That state of incompleteness can be deliberately structured. 'It is a matter of awakening imaginative capacities,' Greene (1994: 3) concurs, 'and of appealing to people's freedom.'

*Free human beings can choose, can move beyond where they are, can ascend to places of which, in their ordinariness, they could have had no idea, and it is **these powers of imagination which artistry can claim.***

Conclusion

O'Neill's drama praxis highlights the ambiguous roles of the leader and participants, roles which are multi-faceted and require the capacity to control, submit, direct and collaborate. Teachers have to find a delicate balance between their own intentions in the drama and those of their students. In other words, 'to lead the way,' as O'Neill says, 'while walking backwards.' Leaders, she argues, will need to act as guides who should 'know where the travellers have come from and the nature of journey so far, so as to help to determine the kind of journey which lies ahead.'

Artistry in process drama releases the leader from the burden of planning and invites the participants to co-create the text based on their own desires, needs and agendas.

Throughout this Introduction, readers will have noted how the contextual circumstances impact upon the development of the work. Process drama is driven by group effort. The participants' experiences captured within The Recruiting Officer will inevitably be different from others' encounters at different places with the same pre-text. This is a reason for including the participants' words, wherever possible, so that readers can have a feel for the data which emerged from the context.

Readers will note how O'Neill responded to these contextual circumstances by revisiting her plan. Her praxis is driven, it seems to us, by this rare capacity to empathise with the participants and to take risks in the process. As a result, participants believe themselves to be in control of the work and responsible for its consummation. In process drama, then, one of the primary outcomes of the journey is the consummated experience of the journey itself.

> *Working from a powerful pre-text, we can harness students' imaginations, create dramatic contexts for learning, provide complex language opportunities and furnish them with significant dramatic experience. With an understanding of dramatic tension and structure, it will be possible to achieve the same dynamic organisations that give form to theatre experience. We must recognise that process drama is a significant dramatic mode, springing from the same dramatic roots and obeying the same dynamic rules that shape the development of any effective theatre event. (Cecily O'Neill)*

Episode One
Finding Form

Episode One
Finding Form

This episode contains four chapters illustrating the central nature of dramatic form which informs O'Neill's artistic sensibility. In identifying the key features of process drama she begins by providing an historical overview of the field known as drama in education. O'Neill covers the terrain of the various philosophical currents and educational imperatives and the competing outlooks of the major practitioners.

It is appropriate that O'Neill's principal mentor, leading educational drama theorist Gavin Bolton, shares with us his own analysis of the features powering her praxis. In a revealing portrait of how an educator's theories evolve over time, Bolton demonstrates the changes that have occurred in O'Neill's writings, from a concern with pedagogical outcomes to a more deliberate concentration on aesthetic principles. It was clear that the 1960s and 1970s promoted an emphasis on pedagogy and the characteristics of successful teaching. If we take a few British book titles we clearly see this emphasis: *Development through Drama* (Way, 1967), *The Drama of History: Experiment in Cooperative Teaching* (Fines and Verrier, 1974), *Learning through Drama* (McGregor, Tate and Robinson, 1977), *Dorothy Heathcote: Drama as a Learning Medium* (Wagner, 1976) and *Practical Primary Drama* (Davies, 1983). In O'Neill's earlier textbook *Drama Guidelines* (1976), co-authored with colleagues from the now defunct London Drama and Tape Centre, we note this concern with learning objectives:

> The long-term aim of drama teaching is to help the student to understand himself (sic) and the world in which he lives. The drama teacher is trying to set up situations within which his students can discover why people behave as they do, so that they can be helped to reflect on their own behaviour. (p7)

This long-term purpose is contrasted with the 'secondary aim' which is described as assisting students 'achieve understanding of and satisfaction from the medium of drama since this is the means by which the primary aim is achieved.' It is perhaps in this latter statement that we began to witness in the 1980s and 1990s an attitude that the drama teacher was not interested in the development of theatre skill: 'But unlike those working in theatre, one is teaching not *for* the aesthetic experience, but *through* it.'

The idea became fashionable that drama education (the term *process drama* did not come into wide currency until the 1990s) was solely concerned with teaching content, not form, and was the source of much controversy in the later twentieth-century. It is perhaps unsurprising that, in an era where concrete propositional knowledge was being ardently sought and discrete attainment targets being promoted, it became much easier for teachers to say they were teaching, for instance, the key elements of Brecht's epic theatre, than students' shifts in understanding while participating in a whole group process drama on war. When checklists for learning become the cherished means of evaluating students' knowledge, it can be quicker to grade factual regurgitation of periods of theatre history than to implicate students in dramatic situations which require human struggle and commitment.

However, in her revealing MA 1978 thesis, 'Drama and Web of Form,' sections of which are published for the first time in this book, readers will clearly find that O'Neill's concern with dramatic form is central to her artistic pedagogy, an interest that was with her from the earliest periods of her research. Form in drama refers to how the medium's key aesthetic elements of time, action and space are organised and interrelated. Teachers are in a far more informed position to operate the aesthetic medium if they work from within the creative event in partnership with their students. While teachers need to have their own sense of technique, it is critical that they do not let their skill predetermine the outcome or squash their students' abilities when making drama.

Often, O'Neill writes, the students may have a firmer grasp on the form than their teacher, they have better intuitive hunches as to what questions might be more fruitfully explored. This is where the leader's ability to step off the page and permit spontaneous encounters needs to be accommodated. O'Neill's study of the work of Beckerman (1970), Dewey (1934), Langer (1953) and other arts philosophers, drama critics and playwrights, honed her concern with structure and spontaneity. If we accept that perceptual abilities can be heightened when participants have a relationship with the material, and permit it to play along with their senses, greater group ownership will emerge.

In *Drama Structures* (1982), which followed the publication of *Drama Guide-lines*, students' artistic sensibilities are heightened. In that text we find a deliberate analysis on how students' responses can influence the direction of the work. *Drama Worlds* (1995) is a fuller testament on how dramatic form is central to process drama. This 1995 book raises the key guiding questions which inform the theatre educator's quest to finding form and are at the heart of the chapters which follow.

> What specific dramatic forms can be drawn on to give substance to the process? What kinds of encounter will yield the most significant experience for the participants in the episode? How can the leader build a framework that is sufficiently flexible to allow each participant to engage in a satisfying complex role? How can the group come to take an increasing share in the essential playwright function and make decisions about the direction of the work? The best guide for both leader and participants in process drama is a strong sense of dramatic form, a grasp of the structural devices by which playwrights through the ages have created significant dramatic experience, and an understanding of the relationship of content to form in the work. (p131)

1

Drama in Education

First published in *Encyclopedia of English Studies and Language Arts* (1994). General Editor: Alan C. Purves with Linda Papas and Sarah Jordan. Vol. I, Scholastic New York, Toronto, London, Auckland, Sydney.

The recognition of the educational power and potential of drama goes back as far as schooling itself. Drama and education have been formally associated since the Renaissance, when training in language, literature, oratory and moral virtues were among educational goals. In schools and colleges today, drama in education is acknowledged as a way of giving students an experience of making and appreciating theatre, as an approach to other subjects in the curriculum and as a source of personal growth.

The power of drama arises from the access to and experience of other roles and worlds it affords. It is direct and immediate, and its medium is the human being. Drama in education is built on the assumption that learning arises from experience of and engagement with a dramatic world, either as a spectator or participant, and from reflection on the roles, issues, situations, and relationships that occur within it. Drama can both communicate experience and give the communicator a greater understanding of the participant.

In giving an account of drama in education, difficulties of vocabulary immediately arise. At college level, drama customarily means the written text, and theatre implies performance. In schools, drama usually refers to informal, improvised enactment of which the goal is not presentation but the experience and satisfaction of the participants. Theatre indicates the more formal study of the techniques of acting and stagecraft, often culminating in

31

a performance in front of an audience. Theatre in this sense is primarily concerned with the acquisition of a body of skills and knowledge, in other words, learning about the subject. As a result, although it may not always be perceived as an essential subject in schools, a theatre curriculum is relatively easy to plan, teach, and evaluate. Drama, on the other hand, indicates an experience valued for its own sake and for the insight, creativity and understanding that arise from the experience. It carries the implication of learning through the subject, and may present difficulties in terms of specifying goals and outcomes.

At the elementary level, the process of drama in education, with improvisation at its heart, originally found its source in children's play and its justification in the principles of child-centred progressive education. In the 1920s and 1930s at Northwestern University, Winifred Ward (1930) established 'creative dramatics' as an important part of the education of children and their teachers. In Britain during the 1940s and 1950s there were similar developments. Spontaneity, creativity, self-expression and personal growth were the goals of drama in education, rather than the acquisition of theatre skills and presentational outcomes. This distinction between drama in education and theatrical presentation was supported by Peter Slade (1954) and his followers. Slade believed that children should find a natural mode of acting through their own dramatic play. Sincerity and absorption were key features, and children's freedom, creativity and delight in this kind of play qualified it to be regarded as an art form in its own right, without reference to adult notions of theatre and performance. In his profoundly influential handbook, *Development through Drama*, Brian Way (1967) reinforced Slade's distinction between theatre and drama in education, and emphasised personal growth and the development of life skills through exercises in concentration, imagination and sensitivity. The effect of these ideas was to weaken the links between drama in education and theatre, and shift the emphasis in the direction of drama as a developmental tool. This distinction, which began as an attempt to balance the values of personal expression and creativity with experience and appreciation of realised art, is now accepted as both limited and limiting. Drama and theatre are not just part of the same continuum, they are the same medium, whether or not they are concerned with presentation to an audience.

In professional theatre, the rediscovery of improvisation in actor training through the ideas of Stanislavski (*An Actor Prepares*, 1936) coincided with an increase in the authority of the director and the interpretive potential of the actor. At the same time, there was a decline in the influence of the playwright and the script over the theatre event. Adapting the techniques proposed by Stanislavski, Viola Spolin (*Improvisation for the Theatre*, 1964) devised a series of more than 200 acting games and exercises. These are intended not only for actor training but also for use with young people and the community. Spolin's exercises continue to be a vital part of drama training programs in many countries, particularly at secondary and college level.

For Spolin, improvisation is both an art form and a living process. Her exercises, although intended for presentation, however informal, stress spontaneity, discovery and interpersonal communication, and seek to elicit and channel these capacities. Spolin's exercises imply a new relationship in which attitudes permit equality between student and teacher. Ideally, the problems and tasks set up by her exercises teach both students and teachers. 'Side-coaching' is an essential part of her system. Here, the function of the teacher is to help the players focus on the task or problem. It offers teachers the opportunity to avoid a directly authoritarian stance and operate instead as guides, facilitators and fellow players. However, the rules of Spolin's games may limit exploration and discovery by defining the area of discovery too rigidly and promoting competition among players. There may be an emphasis on the payoff, the end product.

Theatre Sports

This trend toward display and competition can be seen in the increasing interest in theatre sports at the secondary and college level. These competitive improvisatory games have grown both from Spolin's exercises, the influence of improvisatory theatre ensembles, and the work of Keith Johnstone (*Improv*, 1979). In theatre sports, teams of skilled and resourceful performers exploit the tightrope quality of improvisation, often in response to audience suggestions and within strict rules and time limits. The emphasis is on individual, original and ingenious solutions to the problems posed by other actors or the audience. The results of the actors' efforts are scored by judges, and prizes awarded. These events can provide exciting and original theatre, especially where the actors do not give in to the pressure for a quick and comic pay-off.

Theatre in High Schools

In the high school curriculum, the emphasis is likely to be on introducing students to the skills of production and stagecraft, especially acting and technical theatre. If these skills are taught out of context, by lectures, worksheets and inappropriate testing, the study of the lively, interactive art of theatre may be turned into inert knowledge and become a subject as predictable and routine as many others in the school curriculum. Techniques in any field are always best studied within living contexts.

There is an assumption that students at this level will be ready to perform plays in public. Many high schools present several public performances each year, often including an ambitious musical. Annual theatre festivals are well attended and encourage both display and competition. Disappointingly, theatre teachers rarely use these occasions to connect their work to the wider heritage of theatre. The plays selected are too often drawn from a short list of familiar favourites, and while these may be ambitious in terms of staging and size of cast, they seldom include new or experimental work or any of the great plays of world theatre. The subject matter is unlikely to address any immediate concerns of the players, audience, or community. However, some high school teachers build on their students' skills in improvisation and present pieces that have been partly or wholly devised by them. This kind of presentation may lack the polish of *Annie* or *West Side Story*, but may give students a stronger sense of ownership and achievement. Topics chosen tend to be of considerable personal interest to the students and elicit considerable engagement and commitment. Some high schools regularly present specially selected plays to specific local audiences, to elementary schools for example.

At college level, drama is seen as part of a liberal education, as a preparation for the professional theatre, or as an introduction to graduate study. Both BA and BFA degrees are offered, reflecting this difference in approach. These in turn lead to the MFA degree for those who plan to work in the theatre, and the PhD for those intending to be college teachers. It is really only at this stage that courses are likely to include the history, criticism, and theory of the stage as a significant proportion of the curriculum. The challenges for colleges, as for high schools, is to devise a theatre curriculum that will not merely teach students about theatre but will motivate and empower them in and through theatre, with the right balance of creation, experimentation, performance, criticism, and scholarship.

At each level of education, the assumption is that, when students are involved in drama and theatre, some significant kind of learning occurs. At secondary and post-secondary levels, this learning is likely to be about theatre techniques and practices. In some elementary schools, the acquisition of skills and techniques associated with performance may be emphasised, however inappropriately, at the expense of discovery, exploration and experimentation. Although it is certainly worthwhile for elementary students to begin to learn about, create, and appreciate theatre – especially where the presentation arises out of their own concerns, explorations, and curriculum – learning *through* drama has a great deal more to offer.

Drama in the Curriculum

Drama in education has been identified by many educators and researchers as a powerful and effective medium for promoting learning in the classroom. Wagner (1988) offers a summary of research documenting the significance of drama in education in the development of oral language, literacy, motivation, positive attitudes, and social and cognitive skills. Unfortunately, research suggests that, while teachers accept in principle that drama can help them achieve their goals, a disappointingly large number of teachers rarely or never use drama. The product orientation of many American schools militates against the use of the process of drama, in spite of its effectiveness as a medium for learning.

Since language is the means by which drama is realised, whether presented on stage or improvised in the classroom, it is not surprising that the advantages to be gained from using drama in the language arts classroom are most fully substantiated. As Ken Byron (*Drama in the English Classroom*, 1986) makes clear, drama is a powerful tool for developing language because the classroom context is temporarily suspended in favour of new contexts, new roles and new relationships and, as a result, unique possibilities of language use and development are opened up. Drama has the potential to change significantly the patterns of communication and interaction in a classroom, and the teacher's part in those patterns.

Drama in education is also acknowledged as an effective mode of learning about specific contexts and issues. It can fulfil particular curricular aims and may be used to clarify, enrich, revise, or reinforce areas of the curriculum, for example, in understanding an event in history, interpreting or elaborating on a character or situation in literature, or developing and exercising a specific social or linguistic skill. History and social studies teachers find drama both motivating and illuminating. Drama of this kind may be limited to the kind of simulation or role-play that in reality is little more than an acted-out discussion; in the hands of a confident and experienced teacher it may lead to genuine exploration, discovery and learning.

Process Drama

In the last decade, the goals of creativity and personal growth that were dominant in the 1960s and early 1970s have given way first to an understanding of drama as an essentially cognitive process concerned with the negotia-tion of meaning and, more recently, to a realisation of the essential nature of the relationship between drama in education and theatre. In Britain, and increasingly in the United States, the process of drama in education has been refined and developed as both a powerful medium for learning in the curri-culum and as an art process in its own right.

Difficulties of vocabulary persist even within this area. The subject is known variously as drama in education, educational drama, creative drama, developmental drama, informal drama, role drama or, more recently, process drama. This last term is a useful and increasingly popular one, and it dis-tinguishes this approach from the practice of the more traditional and fami-liar creative dramatics.

Although superficial similarities occur, there is actually a considerable dif-ference between the appearance, content and purpose of a creative drama-tics lesson, one based on improvisation exercises, and process drama. Ap-proaches based on exercises such as Spolin's will be short-term, task-oriented and presentational. Where creative dramatics may focus on the preparation and enactment of a story or other literary source, process drama is concerned with the development of a wider context for exploration, a dramatic world created by the teacher and students working together within the experience.

In process drama, active identification with and exploration of fictional roles and situations are key characteristics, and there is less emphasis on personal growth, theatrical skills, or the recreation and enactment of an existing story. The imagined world of drama involves participants in active role-taking situations in which attitudes, not characters, are the chief concern. It is lived at life rate and obeys the natural laws of the dramatic medium. The goal is the development of students' insight and understanding about themselves and the world they live in through the exploration of significant dramatic con-texts. Parallel aims are the development of students' capacity to engage more deeply with complex roles and situations, an increase in their perception and use of the power of dramatic expression in both the classroom and the theatre, and the growth of an understanding of dramatic form.

This approach, pioneered in Britain by Dorothy Heathcote and Gavin Bolton, is now widely practiced in other parts of the world, notably Canada and Aus-tralia. It is less familiar in the United States. For Dorothy Heathcote, the end product of improvisation is always the experience itself and the reflection that it can generate. Her work rests on the basis of a sound understanding of theatre form. She believes that drama is not merely stories retold in action but concerns also human beings confronted by situations that change them because of what they must face in dealing with those challenges.

One of the striking features of Heathcote's work is her view of the function of the teacher within the lesson. In more traditional creative drama lessons, the teacher typically remains an external facilitator, a side coach, a director, or a loving ally. Heathcote is likely to begin by adopting a role herself. This strategy, known as teacher-in-role, is the one with which Heathcote is most closely identified.

Through the use of teacher-in-role, it is possible to bind the participants together as a group, engage them immediately in the dramatic action, and manipulate language and gesture to establish the nature of the imagined world that is coming into being in order to challenge the participants' usual way of thinking. The strategy of teacher-in-role has been profoundly misinterpreted by those who do not grasp its functional and structural properties. It is never merely acting or joining in on equal terms with the group. For Heathcote, the explicit educational aim of her work in drama is always to build a reflective and contemplative attitude in the participants. She uses the contrasting energy of non-dramatic activities such as writing, drawing, and map-making to enrich and deepen the quality of reflection on the dramatic experience. It is only in recent years that Heathcote's emphases on learning and reflection, the immediacy and significance of the experience, and its essential group nature have become common currency among drama teachers.

Structuring Process Drama
Process drama allows for an extended experimental encounter with the medium. Explorations are never merely brief exercises; they extend over time and include a variety of strategies (O'Neill and Lambert, 1982). Through process drama the dramatic world can be developed episodically or in units of action that develop and articulate aspects of the dramatic world. The structuring process involves the careful sequencing and layering of dramatic units or episodes, often in a non-linear way, which cumulatively extend and enrich a fictional context. The existence of these episodes or units instantly entails structure, since it is the relationship between parts of the work that make it a true process. This relationship is likely to be much more complex than the linear connections of sequence or chronological narrative, where the segments of the work are strung together like beads on a chain rather than becoming links in a web of meaning. In process drama, varying levels of involvement and separation, of participation and detachment, of activity and reflection may be incorporated.

Story Drama

It is not always possible for teachers to operate in the unpredictable and challenging way of process drama, especially those who have had limited training and experience in drama and theatre. A useful approach that shares many of the most significant aspects of process drama is known as story drama. This way of working is likely to be particularly valuable in the language arts classroom and accessible to teachers of even limited experience. David Booth (*Drama Words*, 1987) of the University of Toronto was influential in the evolution of this approach, which can be a bridge for the teacher between more traditional creative dramatics and process drama. Here, the original story or picture book is used as a source of understanding rather than as a subject for dramatic adaptation. It provides a framework for exploration and becomes a springboard for meanings as the participants experiment with roles, meet challenges and solve problems within the imagined world of the story. The teacher may take on a role in order to structure the work from within the experience. The improvisation will focus on a genuine dramatic encounter, and the students' responses and decisions will determine the development of the drama. All the activities that form part of the process of the drama can be used to help students enter the world of the story and respond imaginatively and dramatically to the original text. In doing so, they generate both a new text and a unique dramatic experience.

Drama in Education: Recent Progress

In recent years, there has been a growing recognition that the distinction between drama and theatre is a false one. Drama and theatre are in effect the same medium, whether work is undertaken for the satisfaction and insight it produces for participants or whether it is prepared and presented for an audience. Recent curriculum statements for drama and theatre in schools are likely to define the subject in the following ways: as an art form and a way of knowing; as ways of understanding ourselves and the world around us; as a collaborative and socially cohesive enterprise; as a way of learning other subjects; as a means of encountering and understanding our own and other cultures; and as an opportunity to make and appreciate theatre.

Philosophers, artists, and educators are working to integrate aesthetic considerations and applied curriculum concerns more effectively. In Britain, with the advent of a national curriculum and a new emphasis on precisely defined attainment goals, there has been a similar attempt to redefine the relationship between drama in education and theatre. The task for these theorists and educators is to refine the purposes and outcomes of drama in education without abandoning its exciting and innovative pedagogy.

The gains that have been made in drama in education, in both theory and practice, are enormous. Teachers have begun to understand the essential elements underlying dramatic structure and to employ a wide range of strategies through which either the play text or the developing dramatic world may be explored and articulated. They are able to exploit the power of the dramatic context for the different kinds of learning it may yield. Drama in education can promote knowledge, competencies, insights, and processes that will help students face the countless challenges and opportunities that lie ahead.

2

Process Drama

The following analysis first appeared in *A Conceptual Framework of Classroom Acting* by Gavin Bolton. PhD dissertation, University of Durham, 1997, pp362-374. Sections from this account were later published in Bolton's (1998) text *Acting in Classroom Drama: A Critical Analysis*, Stoke on Trent, Trentham Books.

Cecily O'Neill, who introduced the term 'process drama' into our drama education vocabulary, has long been associated with the work of Dorothy Heathcote, notably since her collaboration with Liz Johnson (1984) in collecting within one volume the writings of Dorothy Heathcote published in international journals over a period of twenty years. This chapter, in attempting to identify defining characteristics of 'Process Drama', will, perhaps inevitably, draw attention to differences and similarities with Heathcote's classroom practice. Two years earlier O'Neill had published *Drama Structures: A Practical Handbook for Teachers* in collaboration with an ex-student of Heathcote's, Alan Lambert (1982).

This book begins unambiguously with 'Drama in education is a mode of learning.' By this date, 1982, although the general public might have needed some persuasion about the validity of this statement, there was a fair guarantee that most of the people likely to read such a book would perceive the assertion by O'Neill and Lambert as familiar rhetoric[1]. Nor would their readers be surprised that the lessons described in the book included the use of teacher-in-role, teacher narration,[2] whole group decision-making, small group tasks, interaction in pairs, the use of depiction, enquiry into issues related to curriculum subjects, moral dilemmas, related written work and art work. What was new for readers was the authors' attempt to show, in considerable detail, patterns of carefully structured dramatic sequences based on Heathcote's methodology and philosophy. Sample examples of 'living

41

through' drama already available in print were to be found in: Heathcote's various journal articles in which she would refer to key moments of a lesson; in Betty Jane Wagner's (1976) analysis, which tended to abstract vivid incidents from lessons to illustrate Heathcote's pedagogy; and my own (Bolton, 1979) publication which tended to use actual classroom practice as illustrative of some theoretical point. O'Neill and Lambert's purpose was rather different. By giving *detailed* reports on lessons they had taught in schools, they sought to help readers identify, not a formula, but guidelines for developing a cumulative process of learning when planning to engage a group of pupils with a topic of interest. Each sequence had been tested with more than one class, so that alternative routes are sometimes included in the account. It is O'Neill's own account of these teaching sessions that will provide the source for this chapter's analysis.

Before Heathcote's work became known, the pattern most familiar to teachers was plot. O'Neill and Lambert see structure as overriding plot, even when the dramatisation is embedded in a time sequence such as their lesson based on 'The Way West'. The authors warn:

> Since this theme has a kind of narrative shape provided by the 'journey', it is important not to allow the linear development of story-line to take over. If it happens, the work may become merely a series of incidents – 'what happened next'. Instead, drama is likely to arise from moments of tension and decision, or when the settlers must face the consequence of their actions. (p41)

Faithfully following Heathcote's search for ways of opening up an understanding in her pupils that every person's action betrays deeper values, the teacher of 'The Way West', in using the device of family photographs, asks one or two pupils to answer the following kinds of questions from their picture frame: 'What are you looking forward to in your new life?', 'What do you fear most in the months which lie ahead?', 'What do you miss?', 'Any regrets?'

Above all, their work derived from a respect shared by Heathcote for how a dramatist works. These practitioners understood, for instance, how the deliberate manipulation of events out of their natural time sequence multiplies the perspectives from which they may be viewed. Looking back or looking forward to an event highlights and makes accessible hues of significance not available if one can only be in the event. The potential for 'living through' drama expands, making a cascade of possibilities if the present embraces the past and the future, if the pain of an event was yesterday or the implication of an event is tomorrow.

O'Neill and Lambert fed this expanded 'living through' into many of their lessons. The creative manipulation of time[3] became part of their dramatist's repertoire. An example from *Drama Structures* is entitled 'Disaster'. Working with pre-adolescents, O'Neill begins the lesson with:

> Twenty-five years ago, in a certain community, a terrible disaster occurred. The way of life of that community was changed forever. The young people of the community who had been born after the disaster decide to commemorate the 25th anniversary by presenting a play about the disaster. They hope this will remind the people of what happened, and will prevent such a disaster from ever happening again.

This class were then invited to select a disaster. They decided that a man-made rather than a natural disaster would be more interesting to explore and chose a nuclear explosion, not due to war but the result of a series of blunders on the part of the government.

O'Neill begins the work on this theme by inviting the class in small groups to show some background to the disaster, such as what errors of judgement were made and how communities were affected by it. These are played without comment, simply supplying images of an event. O'Neill now reverts to her original ploy – the idea of young people born after the event using an art form to commemorate it. Thus the 'living through' mode, the sustained *now*, as it were, *of* the drama is occurring *outside* the time of the incident and yet safely invites concentration on that incident. This example of finding a reason to place the class outside the event in order to look at it could be said to be true to Dorothy Heathcote.

However, and this is my reason for using this particular illustration, Cecily O'Neill drew from her dramatist's palette a colour that Dorothy Heathcote was by the mid-1970's deliberately avoiding. O'Neill describes the next step of her lesson:

> ..the teacher...takes on the role of a visitor from the State Council for the Arts, and tells them that she is very pleased that they are working so hard to commemorate this tragic incident in history. She admires their talent, as well as their effort and dedication. *However* [my italics], *she is slightly unhappy about the way they have chosen to approach their text. They seem to be taking a rather negative view of the whole incident. They also seem to have got their facts wrong. She tells them that it is now known that the disaster was due to the sabotage of one employee, who had become unbalanced due to overwork...* (O'Neill and Lambert, 1982, p183)

43

Gradually, the pupils begin to recognise they are being subjected to a political act of deception which becomes clearer when 'this nice lady from the State Council for the Arts' further suggests that, should they consider changing the form of the commemoration, a great deal of financial support from the Government might be forthcoming. Suddenly, as a direct result of teacher intervention, the pupils find themselves in a play about state repression for which the 'Disaster' was but a pretext – and O'Neill has in this one strategy moved her work in a direction with which Heathcote has less sympathy.

This injection by the dramatist/teacher of dramatic irony into the structure of the sequence is an example of moving the experience towards a new genre for which I may initially have been responsible and to which Cecily O'Neill eventually applied the name 'Process Drama'. It is a predominantly 'living through' experience derived from Heathcote, but crucially independent of her in respect of its theatricality. Within three introductory pages of her later publication, O'Neill (1995: xv and xiii) is able to claim both that 'Process Drama is almost synonymous with the term drama in education' and that it is a 'theatre event.' Significantly, there is no repeat in *Drama Worlds* (1995) of 'Drama in Education is a mode of learning' (O'Neill and Lambert, 1982, p11). It is not that O'Neill is now denying learning outcomes but that, by seeing her brand of drama education as a genre of theatre, the term 'learning' appears too narrow, too limiting, too reminiscent of teaching objectives. In *Drama Structures* (1982) the authors, while struggling towards a new form of 'living through' drama, nevertheless cling to specified learning categories.[4] In *Drama Worlds* (1995) the participants are not treated explicitly as 'learners', but as active agents making theatre happen. O'Neill explains:

> When drama techniques are valued only for their capacity to promote specific competencies and achieve precise ends, and remain brief, fragmented, and tightly controlled by the teacher or director, the work is likely to fall far short of the kind of generative dramatic encounter available in process drama. (p5)

It is the language of theatre that Cecily O'Neill now applies to her study of how process drama works. This is not the traditional language of climax, shape plots and sub-plots but contemporary theatre language of episodes, transformation, ritual, spectatorship, alienation and fragmentation. She is intent, by references to dramatists and theatre theorists, on drawing parallels between the components of a play performance and those of a drama sequence. It is *improvisation*, however, that she sees at the centre of process drama, even though she may employ depiction and scripts as part of the sequence.[5]

I now analyse an example of process drama which seems to epitomise the approach, 'Frank Miller.'

Frank Miller

O'Neill gives two separate versions of this sequence about the return of an exile. The first account, making up the book's Preface, not only gives the reader a flavour of what Process Drama feels like, it also points to a critical feature, that the experience of Process Drama, like any significant event in life, readily lends itself to becoming a narrative. For a participant, in retelling 'what happened to me in our dramatic event', the necessary reformulation into a story becomes a source for new understanding.

This is my analysis of the episodic record shown in the first chapter (O'Neill: 1-3). I will centre on assumptions about the acting behaviour of the participants, drawing attention to O'Neill's own analysis of drama elements where appropriate.

> The leader in role speaks to the whole group and announces that news has come that Frank Miller intends to return to town. What is his purpose in coming back and what action should the townspeople take to protect themselves? There are implied questions about their involvement in Frank's departure ten years previously.

This use of teacher-in-role is exciting and threatening to both teacher and members of the class[6]. The reception of this pre-text with some classes will range from 'cynical' through 'entertained' to 'captivated'. This is the first step in what Heathcote calls 'allurement', when there is a partial, collective mental engagement with the teacher's performance in role. The teacher is signing that she is in a fictitious mode and is inviting the class to join her. The responses, according to O'Neill in her Preface, are unevenly helpful, from 'perhaps it's a joke' to 'he could be out there waiting for us.' It is integral to Process Drama, as indeed to all 'living through' approaches, that elements of this reader response will become incorporated into the subsequent text.[7] The class, however, are readers *framed*. Like it or not, they have been endowed with an incipient role as people with a past who share some kind of relationship with a Frank Miller. To play this game properly, the members of the class are restricted to behaving as if they already own this fiction, a conspiracy of deception, impossible to sustain beyond a few minutes.

> The leader clarifies some of the details that have emerged, and the group decides on further elaborations of time and place.

Relief may be felt by the participants that the conspiracy is temporarily over and they are free to become planners of drama rather than *be* there. This section turns out to be absolutely crucial to the rest of the work, for their decision that they as townsfolk all had a hand in sending Frank Miller to jail ten years previously combines a dramatist's touch with pedagogic genius; in that single decision lies the potential for each member of that class to own[8] Frank Miller, the story and the character. Each person in the room has effectively been given a piece of history which theoretically links him/her with Frank Miller. The possibility for Frank Miller to exist for everyone has begun, although it is, at this early stage, merely a seed of an idea.

> *Working in small groups, the participants create tableaux of a number of moments in the early life of Frank Miller.*

This 'composition', as O'Neill calls it, is an exploration, no doubt quite shallow, of possibilities, a sketching of images to see what appears, but it also represents a commitment, for each sketching publicly scrutinised becomes defendable. The participants own their bit, however sketchy, of Frank Miller's history.

> *Improvised encounters. The students work in small groups as they meet and attempt to identify strangers at different locations in town, sussing out which is Frank Miller.*

The class is in familiar Brian Way territory here. It is an exercise with a single objective, to play at interacting with strangers. It is carried out in small groups simultaneously throughout the room. It may be an unexceptionable example of an exercise structure but, for the first time, the participants are on their feet *being* townsfolk as opposed to *demonstrating* them, using what I have previously referred to as a dramatic playing mode as opposed to performance mode. I suspect that this flavour of being townsfolk was but briefly sustained. Like most exercises of this kind, unsupported by teacher-in-role, its status is such that the teacher avoids underlining its outcome as critical, so that if any participants fail to play convincingly to themselves (and pitfalls abound), there is little loss of face or of drama. The teacher may have wanted it merely to serve as a break from the pressure to be seen to be doing well of the previous exercise. Indeed, however tentative or rough-hewn, it can supply the material for the more serious step to follow:

> *One of these encounters is recreated for the rest of the group, and it emerges that Frank Miller has indeed returned.*

It may be that the connection between this enacted performance of the Sheriff approaching two strangers and the original dramatic playing of that meeting was but slender. It is a typical 'living through' drama ploy that the teacher can take a pedestrian contribution and elevate it into something significant. Dorothy Heathcote is always keen, for example, to write up on a blackboard even the most casual answer to her question, knowing that this changes its status. In this lesson a casual bit of role-playing can suddenly become enhanced by its being selected for demonstration, as though the original dramatic playing was but a sketched outline, a point of reference to be filled out. One can be sure that the incident thus demonstrated takes on unexpected prominence, especially in the instance of O'Neill's lesson, since the person playing Frank Miller, when asked by the Sheriff what his occupation was, answered 'hate.'

> *Working in pairs, in role as past associates of Frank and friend, participants discuss the particular implications of Frank's return. What effect will it have on the lives of those who knew him well or feared him most? Half the group, the confidantes, reflect aloud on the information acquired, their partners listening. The class then select the character who had a son, born soon after Frank had left.*

There are three parts to this item. The role-play in pairs, sharing a worry with a friend, is a more secure exercise than the previous one of assessing whether a stranger could be Frank Miller. The familiarity of the interaction is likely to give the worried one a sense of becoming a character in a play. Immediately afterwards, the responsibility switches to the listeners who feed back to each other (and to the audience of friends) what they have heard. Once more, a piece of role-play is made to be significant, for one group now hear their own words reported back. This confirms their place in the play. However, that confirmation is but temporary, for the teacher wants them to select *one* of these characters. In choosing the Postmistress whose son thinks his father is dead, the group show a sharp sense of what would be dramatic and a mature willingness to cooperate in giving up their individual creations – just as they have been elevated to public acknowledgement. Such a switch of loyalties could be said to be typical of process drama. It is conceivable that for some participants a process of ownership of role had begun, now to be abandoned.

> Returning after a break, the class is invited to participate in a game – Hunter and Hunted, which the teacher sets up as Frank and Sarah (the postmistress). Two volunteers are blindfolded and are required to find/escape each other within a circle of watchers.

Reviving an atmosphere from a previous session can present problems. A game such as the above brings back the *feeling* of what they have been creating, a feeling they could easily lose if new details had been immediately pursued. Central to process drama is the sense of experiencing the fiction[9], even while making decisions about it. The teacher in this sequence wants the class to feel that Frank Miller is *there* as they make up their play about him. In this way it is an overarching 'living through' experience for the participants, even though they may be planning or directing or playing a game.

Narration by the leader to clarify the development of the work so far.

No doubt this narration, while useful for recalling and tidying up details, is also recreating Frank Miller's presence in that room.

The students work in pairs. One is Frank and the other is his son. Frank knows who the boy is, but the son only knows Frank as a stranger.

This moves the drama into a different gear. On the surface it is but another pairs exercise, but it is an advance on any exercise in Brian Way's repertoire. The mode will certainly be dramatic playing, but deception has crept in, which now colours every gesture, every line of dialogue. The actors can enjoy the theatre game of two characters who cannot be explicit, the one because he cannot tell, the other because he does not know. It seems that this theatrical dynamic overrides the disappointment some may have felt that they have dropped their incipient roles for the sake of class consensus. It is possible that ownership of the emerging story is gaining priority over specific role-experience.

This kind of theatre game marks again process drama's departure from Heathcotean principles. Whereas Heathcote might, very occasionally, set up such a scene to be demonstrated for the benefit of scrutineers, she would avoid setting it up as an exercise to be experienced simultaneously in pairs. Process drama seeks such an opportunity, seeing it as central to the creative sequence.

Forum Theatre. Two students volunteer to play the scene where Frank's child tells his mother about his meeting with Frank.

An active audience directs the scene, suggesting dialogue and reactions. An example of collective ownership of the fiction.

A Dream Sequence. The class works in three larger groups, creating a dream in sound and movement for either Frank, Sarah or their son.

Another chance to experience their fiction differently, at a more abstract level of guilt or wishful fantasy or ugly memories, using expressive resources of musical gesture[10] rather than the naturalism of preceding exercises and demonstrated scenes. Here the teacher is electing to tap the thematic thrust of the fiction, temporarily taking its meaning beyond 'who should say what to whom and how someone might feel about it'. When the participants return to naturalism some will carry something of this thematic impulse into it.

> *In threes, the family has a meal.*

Pure improvisation, without an audience. This is another example of the dramatic playing mode elevated through appropriate tension within the structure. More demanding than the equally telling previous scene of Frank meeting his son, for it is a three-way interaction, the experience of which could be seen by the participants as making or breaking the worthwhileness of the whole work. The level of ownership needs to be such that the improvisation both feels authentic and achieves a significant outcome, one worth reporting to the rest of the class. Again, it is a significant part of Heathcote's and O'Neill's approaches that reporting, whether as in this instance to the class or just to one's own diary, is an enhancement mechanism for elaboration or refinement.

> *Three volunteers recreate their scene for the rest of the group. Tensions grow between the characters. Inner voices are added. The scene ends with a threat of violence and the characters trapped in their isolation.*

Once more there is a relinquishing of one's own creation for the sake of selecting one. It seems that the collective passion about themes is to override personal ownership. This is not a criticism of the lesson or of the method. Indeed the alienation built into this requirement to lay one's own pursuit on one side may be regarded as a strength of the experience. Ultimately, it is the spectator component that predominates. Process drama in O'Neill's hands has returned unerringly to Heathcotean objectives.

It is also in Heathcotean style that O'Neill adopts the inner voices as part of the final presentation and again, in the following description of the final episode of the process drama sequence, O'Neill is inviting the participants *as spectators* to confirm what they now understand. 'What did I discover as an actor?', although not without importance, has been overtaken by 'What do we, as audience, now read into the complexities of our Frank Miller situation?'

> *Earlier tableaux are recalled, and each of the Franks is isolated and placed in relationship to the others. One extra figure is added to show Frank as he is at the end of the drama.*

The whole sequence, culminating in this final reflection, has indeed been 'its own destination and the group an audience to its own acts' (O'Neill, 1995: xi).

Theatre has been made. O'Neill's interpretation of 'living through' drama has been sophisticated in its conception and multiformal in its methodology.

Notes

1 By this time there was a growing number, if only a small minority, of Arts education experts, such as Malcolm Ross, David Aspin and Peter Abbs whose theoretical position embracing the idea of a generic base for all the arts downplayed the value of drama as a learning medium.

2 Narration by the teacher in Heathcote's and O'Neill's work had many different functions, but usually avoided dictating actions by the pupils of the kind described by Slade and Way.

3 Cecily O'Neill's fascination with time as a key element in drama emerged in her MA dissertation with Durham University (1978) entitled 'Drama and the Web of Form'.

4 They are (1) Learning arising from content of the lesson: (2) Social learning: (3) Skills and (4) Intrinsic – 'a growth or change in understanding' (p14-15).

5 O'Neill uses the term 'improvisation' broadly to include many kinds of dramatic activities but it is the 'living through' element, that is the use of teacher-in-role to set the scene in order to clarify it or to move it on that gives process drama its dominant (but not consistent) characteristic. She appreciates, of course, that improvisation will be more readily understood by her readers who no doubt see the use of teacher- in-role as but one of many kinds of 'impros' or 'improvs'.

6 I can recall doing this kind of introduction on one occasion when a section of the adult class announced they were all newcomers to the town and therefore had no memories!

7 O'Neill writes that 'It is useful to conceive of the text, whether written, improvised or transcribed, as the 'weave' of the event' (1995: 19).

8 The word 'ownership' is very useful, embracing as it does a mental commodity that may both expand and become more dense. That is, out of the experiences of the drama session, a participant may both acquire knowledge about something and become more responsible and possessive about it. In this example, a participant may learn more about Frank Miller and also identify with Frank Miller. That identifying process may arise from acting, directing or contributing to a discussion. An interesting BEd dissertation by Carol Malczewski of Victoria University, British Columbia (1988) is entitled 'Toward a Theory of Ownership in the Dramatic Process'.

9 This point is brought out well by David Davis in interviewing Dorothy Heathcote who says: 'I would say you are always in the play whenever the mind's image begins to affect how you're feeling about what's going on here...' Davis, David (1985) 'Dorothy Heathcote interviewed by David Davis' in *2D* Vol. 4. No. 2. Spring.

10 To use Jacques-Dalcroze's useful term.

3

Working from Within:
Teacher and the Group as Artists
in the Process

Unpublished paper by Cecily O'Neill and Alan Lambert which identifies some early concerns with teacher-in-role and play (Spring, 1979).

mprovised drama is a group activity. In drama in education, this group will include the teacher. It is becoming clear that the teacher is likely to function most effectively in educational drama from within the creative process, as co-artist with his pupils, rather than remaining on the outside of the work, as facilitator or manipulator.

The idea that the teacher should involve himself in the creative work of his pupils is a fairly recent one. In the 1950s and 1960s, pioneers in educational drama, such as Peter Slade and Brian Way, emphasised the need to foster the creativity of children and allow them the freedom to express themselves through drama. It was assumed that this self-expression is natural growth which would flourish of its own accord and could only suffer from the intervention of the adult. The greater the freedom given to the child, it was thought, the greater would be the creativity which would ensue. In this view of drama, the teacher's function is reduced to that of a facilitator, who perhaps provides the time and space in which the drama occurs, offers an external stimulus or comments on the end-product. The banality and superficiality of much that passes for educational drama, however, has called these assumptions into question. It has become clear that, left to themselves with freedom to create, children create what they already know. Without the teacher to challenge and extend their ideas, it is difficult for children to achieve new insights through drama.

51

If this is the case, where teachers do not exercise their teaching function during the on-going dramatic function, educational effectiveness is likely to be seriously weakened. In order to create situations in drama that will involve pupils in learning, the teacher needs to be part of the creative process from the very beginning of the work. Only then can the teacher understand and create from within. Such leaders in the field of educational drama as Dorothy Heathcote and Gavin Bolton are supremely effective teachers who operate within the drama process, sharing responsibility for the growth of the work, yet influencing and challenging the participants in the drama.

The kind of drama that will allow the teacher the greatest opportunity for effective intervention is likely to be spontaneous improvisation, involving the whole group. In this kind of work, the quality of response will be very different from that in prepared improvisation, even where preparation time is very limited. First, there is no end product or performance in mind, which is to be communicated to others. Since the experience is happening *then* to the group there is no need to repeat it for others, nor would it be appropriate to do so. The pupils are faced with the need to respond immediately within the fictional situation. They are challenged by what takes place. They have to find clues and direction. They have to build on what others have offered, and negotiate the meaning of the work with the teacher and the rest of the group. The teacher will not be looking for any technical skills of presentation or characterisation, but for the qualities of thinking and feeling which the children bring to the drama, and the integrity of response that they reveal. It will soon become apparent which children are able to accept the make-believe, to initiate ideas for the group, and to respond and to build on the ideas of others.

In this kind of work, the most effective channel for intervention by teachers, and the easiest way for them to engage directly in the creative process with the pupils, may be adopting their own role in the drama. By doing so, teachers will be putting themselves inside the creative process, where they can, without distorting the progress of the drama, challenge pupils' thinking, support any contributions to the work, move the drama on and, most important, stand in the way of facile solutions by slowing down work which may be moving too fast. By adopting the right kind of role, the teacher can control, guide, and shape the lesson from inside, in a way that is economical, educational, and aesthetic.

For many teachers, to adopt a role in the drama and involve themselves as a co-artist with their pupils may be neither easy nor immediately successful. Teachers must be prepared to surrender the usual role as teacher, in which they are seen as the final arbitrator and the chief source of knowledge. This may pose difficulties for teachers whose view of themselves is inflexible or whose confidence is easily shaken. Teachers may also feel that they lack the necessary acting skills to employ this method successfully. Most important of all, the teacher may be unable to tolerate the uncertainty, spontaneity and risks that are involved in this way of working. But, with perseverance, all these problems can be overcome.

If the work is seen to be enjoyable and successful by the group, the teacher's effectiveness is strengthened. The use of the role does not imply great acting skill, since what it requires is not so much the creation of a fully rounded character as the adoption of an attitude. What is absolutely essential is commitment to the make-believe, if teachers are asking for the belief and involvement of the children they themselves must believe fully. A class unused to this way of working may greet a first attempt with laughter or embarrassment, and these may be reactions to the newness of the method or a test of the teacher's commitment to it. The children may be testing the teacher before going along with the whole idea and taking the risk of offering a response to the teacher's role.

Once the children have begun to respond, the teacher must genuinely respect their contributions, even if they go against the teacher's own logic, or are based on the children's limited and inaccurate understanding of the situation. Even the smallest contributions must be heard and given support. The child who, in a drama about the Pilgrims, claims to have a photograph of his (sic) birthplace with him, has made a serious contribution to the work that should be accepted. The anachronism can be dealt with later. It is important that such offerings are not dismissed as inaccurate or irrelevant, and they must be accepted in a positive and supportive way. The deliberately destructive and facile response is usually recognisable, and can be tactfully ignored, challenged or put to some use. The children may laugh at this kind of response, but the teacher must not. A glib and mocking attitude in the teacher is likely to produce the same kind of response in the class and will effectively destroy any hope of depth in the work.

If the teacher is about to use this method for the first time, it is wise to explain to the class what the method will involve and to try out some short examples in order to establish the rules of the game. The teacher may test the class on their ability to pick up clues from what he or she says, and respond to them by initiating several brief scenes. The teacher may be a parent- 'What time did you get home last night?' – a policeman – 'What were you doing in that empty house?'– a shop assistant – 'Well, madam, have you decided which dress you'll take?' and so on. After the children have understood these simple beginnings, it may be possible to initiate a piece of work which has potential for real development.

The beginning of the work must be clear and direct, and may be preceded by discussion of an agreed theme. Though the development of the work may depend on how the teacher shapes the contribution of the group within the growing situation, the beginning of the work is the teacher's responsibility. Initial statements in role should be strong and simple – additional information can be added once the drama has started:

> Listen carefully. This wagon train will be leaving soon, on the first stage of our journey to Oregon. I am wagon master on this trip, and I must make certain that all the wagons are properly equipped before we start.

This statement, offered in role, might be used to introduce a lesson on the westward migration in the United States in the nineteenth century. The class, through its responses and questioning, will ask for whatever else it needs to know. It is not necessary to have researched the theme in depth before the drama begins. The motivation for research may arise from the work and the class will quickly identify what it is that they need to know. Since this is not a history lesson, truth or response in the thinking and feeling is more important at this point in the work than historical accuracy.

The teacher who is new to this way of working may find it easier at first to adopt an authority role, through which control is likely to remain in their hands – the chief, the expert, the official, the gang boss, the warden, the captain – all of these roles are not too far removed from the normal role as teacher. As teachers become more accustomed to this way of working, they can adopt the kind of role which allows them to play a part in initiating the action, but then permits them to step back from the centre of the action and hand over responsibility to the children. Roles such as the messenger, the outsider, the apprentice, are likely to build the status of the class and be the most effective strategy for entering the creative process with the children, but it must be seen as only one among many such strategies, and used when appropriate. Its real value is that it allows teachers to become a co-artist with their pupils, so that together they can forge the developing meaning of the work.

In the encounter of drama, the articles and their materials are one and the same. The people in the drama are not only creators, but also the means by which the drama is created. So, in educational drama, it may be possible to regard the teacher at one moment as an amalgam of playwright and director, with the group as living tools and materials. At another time the children may be operating as the artists and the teacher, working in role, may be material which they can manipulate, but which will impose its own restraints on the work and possesses its own essential qualities, like any other medium. Alternatively, both teacher and group may share the creative impulse.

Like any creative thinking which ventures into new territory, the drama teacher takes considerable risks. It may be very difficult for teachers to go ahead in a situation where no elaborate plans can be made for the future, and over which they do not possess complete control. Teachers have to learn to think on their feet, holding a number of possible choices for action before the inner eye. Each new stage of work will present decisions that could not have been foreseen clearly at an earlier stage. The teacher is working in a kind of open possibility. In this situation, fraught with uncertainty, the fear of losing control of the work may cause teachers to be intolerant of the independent growth of the process and of their pupils' independent contributions.

However, the teacher is not entirely without support in the venture into unknown territory. First, as teachers become more skilled in structuring and controlling the work from inside, by the use of role and the understanding of structure, they are in fact acquiring technique. They gain this technique only through experience in working through the process, since advances in technique will only arise from effort to solve whatever problems grow out of experience. But even as the teacher gains in skill, he or she must not allow the work to become predictable and lose the sense of something new in the making. The second support to teachers in this work is their own effectiveness as a model for pupils' behaviour. As has been pointed out, the teacher's own commitment to the work must be complete. It is the teacher, as leader, who will create the atmosphere for the make-believe and, to some extent, establish the rules for its development. The teacher will be indirectly demonstrating appropriate behaviour and reactions to the pupils, through cues of speech and gesture.

The third support to the work is that the contributions of the children themselves will not be without inner structure. Although their purposes will be different from the purposes of the teacher, their activities will still be rule-directed. These rules will not be the rules of art or theatre, but the rules of play. The activities of make-believe play and drama have a great deal in common, as commentators have noted. Both require that the children engage in 'pretend' in regard to objects and situations, both involve the adoption of a role, and both demand interaction. The imaginary play situation will always contain rules of appropriate behaviour although, as in spontaneous improvisation, these will not be formulated in advance. Spontaneity, in play or art, does not imply the absence of rules. In both play and drama, the children will be bound by the constraints of the structure in which they are working. Children will be striving to find the appropriate language and behaviour for pirates, missionaries, scientists, or whatever the context of the drama demands. The skills which children need before they can engage in the drama process, and the rules which will govern their behaviour within the process, are not acting or theatre techniques, but the skills and rules of play.

Although they work together as co-artists in the developing process of drama, the purposes of the teacher and of the pupils will be different. The play for the children will provide an equivalent of make-believe play, and will include the intention to create something. The teacher's purpose will be to structure a learning experience for pupils, through which they may achieve a change in understanding about themselves and the world they live in. The teacher may have the primary responsibility for structuring the work, but that is not to say that the children, as they begin to grasp the possibilities and satisfactions of working in the art form, cannot also contribute to the development of the group's ability. This will not be achieved by a sterile preoccupation with practicing skills or technique outside the drama, but by using the group's existing play skills and sense of rules, and involving them directly in the art form, as co-artists, with shared responsibility for the direction and meaning of the work.

Where there is collective agreement to a particular context of make-believe, the process of creative drama has begun. Any contribution by the children or teacher must be accepted, understood and incorporated into the action if it is to have meaning. This active understanding, acceptance and response within the creative process is the negotiation of meaning that is at the heart of educational drama.

4

Drama and the Web of Form

Extracts from 'DRAMA AND THE WEB OF FORM: An attempt to isolate the elements of aesthetic form and their operation within the process of educational drama', MA Thesis by Cecily O'Neill, University of Durham, 1978.

Form in Art and Experience
Form in Art

Philosophers and aestheticians, in all ages, have felt that 'form is the distinctive and precious value of art' (Stolnitz, 1960). Every work of art is held to possess some principle of form or coherent structure and, if a work of art is to be created or apprehended, there must be an awareness of the presence of form in the work. Kant holds that it is the perception of finality or pattern in an object, and the resulting pleasure that is expressed when we say of an object that it is beautiful. For Kant (1951), pure aesthetical judgment is essentially concerned with form. Our experience of the work of art, completed or in the process of completion, will only be fully aesthetic if it is accompanied by this perception of form.

But form in art, in spite of its significance, is not necessarily an obvious quality. It may be the most subtle aspect of the work and the perception of it may demand a most exact attention. Santayana (1958) asserts that to enjoy the value of form requires specifically aesthetic insight and it is precisely this aesthetic insight which must be cultivated if we are to achieve aesthetic experience – 'the crystallisation of significance out of chaos' (Parsons, 1970). Aesthetic experience will arrest our attention and command our effort. Bruner (1962) sees the search for form as a departure from a habitual and literal way of looking, hearing and understanding, so that the ambiguities of a work of art may be resolved. An effort must be made to achieve a new connection between different perspectives. Bruner sees the experience of art as a mode of knowing, one which frees us from the forms of instrumental knowing which comprise the centre of our awareness, and which profoundly complements the knowing of science.

Read (1931) regards the apprehension of form in the aesthetic experience as intuitive in origin, not in any way an intellectual product but 'emotion directed and defined'. Warnock (1976) agrees that our appreciation of form does not come from the intellect but sees its origin in sensation. The nature of the form has to be perceived internally in the object, rather than understood intellectually.

Arnaud Reid (1961) insists that in the experience of art we become in some sense detached from ordinary practical ways of looking at things, and that this detachment is the condition of a new and concrete experience – aesthetic experience. Feeling and cognition are inextricably involved in our attention to the work of art and are incorporated in aesthetic understanding. For Arnaud Reid, feeling plays a supreme part in the ordering and disciplining of human understanding. He holds that there is a cognitive perspective

> which is attainable not so much by going beyond or outside the art itself, as by going deep down inside it. It is an expansion of outlook by cultivation of aesthetic depth, an increase of understanding through the feeling of the involved mind-and-body. (1969)

Vygotsky (1971) echoes this view when he declares that 'Art is the work of the intellect, and of a very special emotional thinking'.

Since aesthetic experience involves both feeling and cognition, form will not be the only thing to be apprehended in a work of art. Just as matter always has *some* form, so form will always be of some matter. We would not follow Heine in declaring that 'In art, form is everything, and material is of no importance.' Although, as Vygotsky (1971) points out, 'to violate the form is to destroy the work of art'. Form in its full significance does not exist outside the material of which it consists. Relations and proportions depend on the material to which they refer. Like Vygotsky, Arnaud Reid (1961) rejects the formalist approach to art. For him, the weakness of the formalist approach is that it identifies art with only one (but relatively superficial) aspect of the work of art:

> The strength of formalism is its affirmation of the central importance of form, and its repudiation of loose association and crude forms of expressionism. Its error is in mistaking pattern, a thin abstraction of form – for the true, robust, artistic form, which is possessed by aesthetic embodiment of feeling. (Reid: p62)

As he points out, his use of the word 'embodiment' stresses the importance of the actual material medium. The embodied meaning is incarnate in the form and, ideally, form and content should be considered as one. Although it is impossible to abstract form from content in a single work of art, it should be possible to define the nature of form in art and to isolate certain general principles of form that will hold true for art generally.

Defining Form

Form is one of the most ambiguous words in the language of art and resists any attempts at simple definition. The dictionary definition is 'shape, arrangement of parts, visible aspect,' and Read (1931) tells us that the form of a work of art is precisely this. There is form as soon as there is shape, as soon as there are two or more parts gathered together to make an arrangement. But form in art does not mean the same as mere geometric shape; this is too narrow a definition to be of much value even in considering visual art alone. Form has to do with the total interrelations of parts, the overall organisation of the work, rather than the mere outward configuration. It consists of sensory elements that have been chosen from a particular medium, and exists only in their interrelations. So form is not some kind of independent container for these sensory elements but, as Stolnitz (1960) has described it, 'a web organising the materials of which it is made' (p27).

Stolnitz has distinguished four common meanings of form in art, and defines them as follows:

1. The organisation and interrelation of those elements of the medium included in the work.
2. The organisation of expressive significance in the work.
3. Form as used to refer to an already known and specific pattern of organisation (e.g., the sonnet form, the concerto.)
4. Form used in a descriptive or eulogistic sense.

It is Stolnitz's first definition of form that will be considered here, and applied to the process of educational drama.

When we speak of the particular form of an individual work of art, we refer to its own unique mode of organisation and not to the type of organisation that it shares with other works of art. Our aesthetic response to such a work will not be to a single aspect but to the inner organisation, the form. This form will not be something prefabricated or superimposed but will originate in some sense in the act of creation so that our aesthetic response will be to form and substance, as one.

Form in Experience

The perception of form, though crucial to the appreciation and creation of art, need not be, of itself, aesthetic. Experience that is not aesthetic can also be possessed of form. Vygotsky (1971), quoting Kohler's psychological experiments with animals, has shown that the perception of form is quite an elementary act and not necessarily aesthetic. The Gestalt school of psychology also recognised that forms which are conceded to have aesthetic value often resemble those toward which everyday perception is biased. Dewey extends these views. In *Art as Experience* (1934) he suggests that, in order to understand art, we should turn to the 'ordinary forces and conditions of experience' (p56). These, he feels, can give us clues to the intrinsic nature of the aesthetic experience, which should not be isolated or disconnected from other modes of experiencing. In order to understand the aesthetic in 'its ultimate and approved forms' (p123), it is necessary to find the sources of art in human experience. Art, for him, is prefigured in the very processes of living.

It is not in the mere flux and change of man's interaction with his environment that Dewey sees the sources of art, but in what he defines as *an* experience. The characteristics *of* experience, for Dewey, are that it begins with an 'impulsion' of the whole organism, outward and forward. The organism moves to satisfy a need, but the nature of this notion is determined by the environment and the past experiences of the organism. Experience occurs continuously, but often remains inchoate. In contrast,

> we have *an* experience when the material experienced runs its course to fulfilment. Then and then only is it integrated within and demarcated in the general stream of experience from other experiences. A piece of work is finished in a way that is satisfactory; a problem receives its solution; a game is played through; a situation... is so rounded out that its close is a consummation and not a cessation. Such an experience is a whole and carries its own individualising quality and self-sufficiency. It is *an* experience. (my emphasis, p132)

Later, he explains that when experience is satisfactory, when it combines memory of the past with anticipation of the future, when it is an achievement of the organism in the environment in which it functions, in other words, when it is unified and consummatory, it is an aesthetic experience.

Dewey is attempting to show that the aesthetic is not some rarefied and ideal quality, but 'the clarified and intensified development of traits that belong to every normally complete experience' (p78). This, he feels, is the only secure basis for aesthetic theory.

Dewey sees form as a character of every experience that is *an* experience. In every such experience, there is form because there is dynamic organisation. The organisation is dynamic because there is growth-inception, development and fulfilment. Langer (1957) seems to agree that works of art will have characteristics symbolically related to those of life itself, and defines living form – 'the expression of human consciousness' in art, as dynamic form, a form 'whose permanence is really a pattern of changes'.

It is this notion of dynamic form that is likely to be of most use in considering form in drama. There is no end product, no work of art to be analysed, only a continuing process which is likely to have 'inception, development and fulfil-ment.' Drama, if it fulfils these conditions, which seem to correspond closely with Aristotle's ideas of 'beginning, middle and end,' is likely to be *an* ex-perience, and therefore to possess form. Dewey (pp137-138) rejects the idea that form is found exclusively in objects which have been labelled works of art, and points out that there is an inevitable tendency to arrange events and objects with reference to the demands of complete and unified perception. Art organises experience more meaningfully and coherently than ordinary life permits. It is, in fact, experience in its most articulate and adequate form.

Form, in both art and experience, he defines as follows:

> Form may be defined as the operation of forces that carry the experience of an event, object, scene and situation to its own integral fulfilment. The con-nection of form with substance is thus inherent, not imposed from without... The problem of discovering the nature of form is thus identical with that of discovering the means by which is effected the carrying forward of an experience to fulfilment. When we know these means, we know what the form is.

Dewey sees the arts as sharing a common form to the extent that they are all organised toward a unity of experience. Aesthetic experience is the paradigm of all experience and, rather than isolating us from ordinary experience, it should help us to understand experience more fully. In interpreting our ex-perience in the world, we will use the same kind of imaginative ordering, the same mixture of feeling and cognition, which play a focal role in aesthetic experience.

Both Stolnitz's first definition of form in art and Dewey's definition of form in experience will be crucial in considering the existence of form in the drama process. Examining the 'organisation and interrelation of the elements of the medium' should enable us to study the way in which the elements of drama are organised. It may be possible to isolate the principles of form which drama shares with other arts and those that are unique to itself. The relationship of theatre to drama may emerge more clearly from an examination of those elements of form that they share. The static nature of Stolnitz's definition, which is perhaps more obviously applicable to existing works of art, will be counteracted by that of Dewey. This should add the sense of the dynamic operation of form in carrying forward an experience to its consummation.

Co-artists: Forging the Form

I have considered drama from the outside, in an attempt to distinguish the operation of form within the work. But, as Witkin (1974) points out, when seen from the inside, such regularities are purely determined and controlled by the aesthetic impulse. Since drama is a group activity, this impulse will be determined, not by a single artist, but by the group. It is within the group experience that meaning is negotiated and embodied, in a form forged by the operation of the group.

In educational drama, the group will include the teacher who is, in the kind of drama I have been considering, to involve him or herself directly with the children in the creative process. As leader, the teacher may provide the primary creative impulse for the group. The drama teacher is not unique in working in this way. Ehrenzweig (1967) points to such artists as Duke Ellington in jazz and Merce Cunningham in modern dance, who possess a supreme ability to make creative use of other people's cooperation. They are artists who work through others. The good art teacher will also work through the pupils, using them, in Ehrenzweig's phrase, 'as his (or her) brushes'.

Creative drama is a spontaneous encounter – a 'genuine existential predicament' (Steinberg, 1972), in the same way that, for the action painter, the canvas provides an arena in which to act, and the image which results in 'an encounter between the artist and his (or her) materials' (Rosenberg, 1962). In the encounter of drama, the artist and his or her materials are one and the same. As Beckerman (1970) declares, 'Man (sic) is not only the creator, but the means'. Depending on the emphasis of the work, it may be possible to regard the drama teacher as an amalgam of playwright and director, with the group as living tools or materials; at another time, the children may be operating as artists and the teacher may be the material they work with, a material which they can manipulate but which will impose its own restraints on the work and possess its own essential qualities, like any other medium. Alternatively, both teacher and group may share the creative impulse, and be co-artists in the development of the work.

The idea of teachers involving themselves in the creative work of their pupils is a fairly recent one. In drama teaching of the 1950s and 1960s, the emphasis was on the necessity of unlocking the creativity of the child. It was assumed that the child develops from the inside out and that the teacher must refrain from interfering with the child's own vision. This approach has a lengthy parentage in educational philosophy, from Plato through Rousseau, and is one that many of the most influential writers on drama have espoused. Teachers whose initial training may have been less than adequate could find comfort in this approach. Their task became the relatively simple one of facilitating the natural self-expression of the child.

The superficiality and banality of much that passes for educational drama has called these assumptions into question. For Robert Witkin (1974: 169-170) the fundamental contradictions of arts teaching arise because arts curricula and arts teaching remain 'external to the pupil's expressive acts.' He claims that teachers of the arts do not understand the nature of the creative process and that this lack of understanding limits their role to a facilitative-inhibitory one. He believes that, to the extent that teachers do not exercise the teaching function during the ongoing dramatic process, their educational effective-ness is seriously weakened. So long as teachers' praxis remains external to the pupils' expressive act, they will have relinquished reflective control of the medium. Teachers need to enter the creative process from the outset, from the very inception of the work. Witkin suggests that teachers can do this 'by controlling and developing the structural demands made in respect of the pupils' unique experience.' They can only discipline the creative act from inside the work.

Although in educational drama they may be sharing responsibility for the development of the work, the teachers' purposes will be different from those of the children. The teachers' educational purposes will be likely to shape their efforts within the process, as they try to focus the work in order to achieve what Bolton (1977) calls 'intrinsic learning' (p71). Bolton points out that teachers are likely to achieve this intrinsic learning for the group by work-ing towards the art form. But, as both Witkin and Bolton show, they cannot do this from outside the process, or in a way which distorts the purposes of the co-artists, the children. The experience must retain its integrity and, like any other artists, both teachers and their groups must follow the guidance of their materials.

There is an aesthetic necessity perceived by artists as they operate with their materials. Creation is a self-correcting process in which artists constantly redirect their aims. Any creative structure will contain unknown variables, which creative thinkers must be prepared to accommodate in the work without losing precision. Rosenberg (1962) describes the artist as working in a kind of 'open possibility,' which he follows Kierkegaard in calling 'the anguish of the aesthetic' (p42). The artist must therefore be able to tolerate his or her own anxiety as well as a degree of ambiguity. In Rosenberg's words, 'to maintain the force to refrain from settling anything, he (or she) must exercise in (him or her self) a constant No'.

As Dewey (1934) has noted, a rigid predetermination of an end-product leads to the turning-out of a mechanical or academic product: 'Like the scientific enquirer, the artist permits the subject-matter of his (or her) perception, in connection with the problems it presents to determine the issue, instead of insisting upon its agreement with a conclusion decided in advance.'

Although the end result may not be foreseen, Ehrenzweig points out that each stage of the work will impose new choices and decisions that could not have been foreseen at an earlier stage. He regards utter watchfulness as the first demand of craftsmanship, a split-second reaction to innumerable variables which may enforce a subtle change of plan (p75).

Bruner (1962) sees the freedom to be dominated by the object as one of the conditions of creativity. What is true of the object is also true of the creative process. One externalises a creative work, permitting it to develop its own being, its own autonomy. To be dominated by an object of one's own creation is 'to be free of the defences that keep us hidden from ourselves' (p16). If it does not in some sense take over, the process is likely to be contrived and alien. A successful art product or process will develop an independent life of its own. To accept the work's own creative life requires humility, which is an essential part of creativity. An artist who is bent on maintaining full control over his or her work is incapable of accepting that a work contains more than he or she consciously puts into it. As Ehrenzweig says, it has an 'otherness' which the artist must be prepared to accept (p123).

It may not be easy for teachers to involve themselves as co-artists in the creative process with the children. First, they must be prepared to surrender the usual role of teacher, in which they are the final arbiter and the source of knowledge. They must be able to share the responsibility both for the creative process and the learning with the rest of the group. This means that they must respect the contributions of the children. As we have seen, if they are to work as artists, they must be prepared to tolerate their own spontaneity and that of the group. Like any creative thinker venturing into new territory, they risk chaos and fragmentation in the work (*ibid*: 160). It may be difficult for teachers to go ahead in a situation in which they cannot make elaborate plans for the future. They must learn to tolerate considerable loosening in their planning and be prepared to remain one step behind in their efforts to keep some measure of control over the work.

As Ehrenzweig (1967: 49) points out, the creative search involves holding before the inner eye a multitude of possible choices. If the teacher is providing the primary creative impulse for the group, it may be difficult for him or her to avoid foreseeing the development of the work. But the teacher must keep his or her intentions flexible, in order to accommodate both the contributions of the group and the internal growth and autonomy of the work. Ehrenzweig (1967: 117) claims that it is the underlying fear of losing control which causes the teachers' intolerance of the independent life of the work of art, and of the their pupils' independent contributions.

However, teachers are not entirely without support in this venture into unknown territory. First, as they become more skilled in using formal elements in structuring the work, they are, in fact, acquiring technique. Dewey (1934) says, 'technique is neither identical with form, or wholly independent of it. It is, properly, the skill with which the elements constituting form are managed'. Technique should not become obtrusive, but should remain in the service of the work itself. Witkin (1974: 45) recognises that 'forms empty of feeling can arise simply by virtue of our capacity to grasp and reproduce external regularities'.

When teachers begin to rely too heavily on technique, their skill in organising the elements of form in the work is likely to become mere virtuosity, which may interfere with the integrity of the experience. The work will become predictable and the sense of 'something new in the making' (Reid, 1961: 49) will be lost. As Dewey (1934: 141) suggests, advances in technique will arise from efforts to solve problems that grow out of the need for new modes of experience. Reid (1961) agrees that the artist is consumed by technical problems. He echoes Ehrenzweig (1967) in suggesting that the artist works in a way that is 'purposive and yet blind.' It is this partial blindness to the outcome of the work that the drama teacher must be prepared to tolerate.

The second support to teachers in this work is their own effectiveness – as a model for pupils' behaviour. It is they who will create the atmosphere of the work and, to some extent, establish the rules of development. Educationalists have long been aware of the importance of the teacher as model, and the research of such play theorists as Singer (1973), Isaacs (1935) and Smilansky

(1963) strongly supports this view. In the realm of art, both Witkin and Ehrenzweig (1967) have stressed the significance of teachers as artists, working alongside their pupils and indirectly demonstrating appropriate behaviours and reactions. So, in drama, the cues of speech and gesture that teachers convey to the pupils from within the process will be crucial.

The third support to the work is that the contributions of the children themselves will not be without inner structure. They will be engaging in what Bolton (1978) has called 'dramatic playing.' In this mode, although they may not be consciously concerned with the problems of form, their activities will still be rule-directed. These rules will not be the rules of art or theatre but the rules of play.

The activities of play and drama have a great deal in common. Both require that the children engage in 'pretend' in regard to objects and situations, both involve the adoption of a role and both demand interaction. Like play, drama is not altogether unreal as are fantasy or fiction but is separate from the reality of everyday life. Both play and drama involve acting-on something or someone that the player does not fully dominate, and both occur within their own boundaries of time and space. In her description of play, Reilly (1974) clearly shows the similarities between the two activities. 'The as-if of the metaphor, the contradiction of the paradox and the specificity of rule are the realities of its substance. (In play, one) accepts and anticipates the pleasure of encountering the unknown' (p144). In the action of both play and drama, through metaphor and rule, reality is explored so that the rules of how things, events, ideas and people operate may be made clear.

According to Huizinga (1955), the more play bears the character of this searching for rules, the more fervent it will be. Erikson (1963), Piaget (1962), and Mead (1934), all stress the importance of rules learned in play, and their application to life. Mead insists that the self emerges in terms of organised group experience. The child must be able to understand and adopt the attitudes of all the others in the game if he or she is to play effectively. This seems to come close to the neo-Freudian theory that all human intercourse involves the projection of scattered parts of oneself into another person. Drama implies this kind of projection, and is also an organised group experience with internal unstated rules, in which a child cannot fully engage unless he or she understands the attitudes of the rest of the group. Spontaneity, in either play or art, does not imply an absence of rules.

Creative work is not limited by rules that exist in advance. It creates its own rules that may only be known after the work is finished. It would be idle to

attempt to anticipate all the moves that open up as the rules are being formulated. For Vygotsky (1933) there is no such thing as play without rules. In
play, the child's freedom is illusory. Far from being an opportunity for freedom, play creates demands on the child to act against immediate impulse.
The imaginary situation will always contain rules of appropriate behaviour,
although these will not be formulated in advance. Like the artist, the child is
bound by the constraints of the structure in which he or she is working. The
skills which children need before they can engage in the drama process, and
the rules which will govern their behaviour within the process, are the skills
and rules of play.

But although the process of educational drama will make special demands on
the group, it will also allow the participants a special kind of freedom. It is an
activity in which they can, in Britton's (1970) terms, be both spectator and
participant at the same time. Although they are the agents of the drama – 'the
makers of the future' – they are also, in some sense, receiving the embodied
meaning of the work almost as an audience would. In the drama, they must act
and decide, in response to the demands of the situation. But, since the situation is a make-believe one, they are free to reflect on and evaluate their actions,
and to 'contemplate forms – the formal arrangements of feelings and events
and ... of ideas, and the forms of language ... in which the whole is expressed'
(p72). As Bolton (1978) suggests, 'the participant is watching himself in some
aspect deliberately singled out from the world around him' (p73). This freedom, of almost simultaneous action and reflection, is unique to drama.

At first, as I have said, the purposes of the teacher and of the children working
within the drama process will be different. Bolton (p5) defines these different
purposes thus: the play for the children provides the equivalent of child's play,
plus the intention to create something. The teacher's purpose is to structure
a learning experience. The integrity of the experience will depend on the way
in which these purposes fit together. As we have seen, the responsibility for
finding the form may be primarily the teacher's. But that is not to say that the
children, as they begin to grasp the possibilities and satisfactions of working
in the art form, cannot also contribute to the structuring of the experience.

The effective drama teacher will make sure that he or she 'educates the
creative power of his executants', in Ehrenzweig's (1967: 113) phrase. This will
not be achieved by a sterile preoccupation with practicing skills or techniques
outside the drama but by using the group's existing play skills and sense of
rules and involving them directly in the art form, as co-artists with shared
responsibility for the direction and development of the work.

When there is collective agreement to a particular context of make-believe, the process of creative drama has begun. As Bolton (1977) has shown, the activity must be not only collective but 'congruent' (p8). The feeling quality of the work must be congruent in its subjective and objective meanings, in the view of the participants. Any contribution to the work, whether by the children or the teacher, must be accepted, understood and incorporated into the action by the whole group, if it is to have meaning.

This process of acceptance and response is not unique to drama. As Child (1969) has said about improvised music: 'the music produced by one player is answered or accompanied by another. This response presumably should make sense, and should provide to the first player an immediate impression that his (sic) music has or has not been understood by the other' (p87). This active, understanding, acceptance and response is the negotiation of meaning which is at the heart of educational drama.

The following is an example of how a teacher structured work in drama, over two sessions, bearing in mind the organising principles of time, tension, and rhythm. The children have asked to explore life in Nelson's navy. The teacher chooses to begin the drama at the point where the group have been seized by a press-gang and thrown into the hold of the ship. Taking the role of bo'sun, the teacher works inside the drama with the children, from the very beginning.

Action	Orientation
In the Hold The Bo'sun explains that the ship is already out of sight of land, and there is no escape. He explains what their duties will be. The group tell each other how they came to be press-ganged.	*The Present* The past is left behind forever, the future is still unknown. There is tension in the setting-up of the rules of the game. Individual roles grow slowly.
On Deck The group work at tasks set by the Bo'sun. The emphasis of the work is on physical rather than verbal activities.	*The Present* Expectations and attitudes are established. The tension of the previous segment is partially relaxed, through the rhythm of physical tasks.
In Port The rest of the crew go ashore, but the new recruits are confined to the ship, since they may try to escape. They are permitted to write home, and this will be the first news their families have had from them. Some include drawings of the ship.	*The Past* A reminder of the homes and families that have been left behind. Reflection on what has taken place in the drama. Here, a different kind of attention is required.

The end of the first session. In the second session, the teacher is in role as one of the sailors, and chooses the first activity to recall to the group the work which has already taken place.

On Deck
In small groups, the class prepares and shows to each other an incident that has happened on board ship.
The harshness of the life of a sailor is made clear, and several of the sailors incur the wrath of the officers.

The Present
This segment recalls what has gone before, and re-establishes the situation for the children. Possibilities for the development of the work are noted by the teacher.

In the Fo'castle
The sailors amuse themselves playing cards and dice. Each has kept some memento from their past life, and tells the rest of the group about it. One sailor has his baby daughter's tooth, another a necklace for his wife, another, anachronistically, a photograph.

The Past
The objects imagined and described by the group establish their past lives. This feeds the feeling quality of the work.

On Deck
The sailors at their tasks. A message circulates among them that there will be a secret meeting at midnight.

The Present – with anticipation of the immediate future.
Tension builds in what is at first an ordinary working atmosphere.

In the Fo'castle
It is time for the meeting. The sailors creep from their bunks, and go to the meeting place. They must decide what to do about one of their number, who has been placed under arrest and is threatened with hanging.

The Present – with a powerful orientation toward the future.
What will be the consequences of a decision to mutiny? The climax of the work.

In the Fo'castle
The men return to their bunks. Each must make his or her own decision. Everyone dreams of the coming of mutiny, and lives their dream through in movement. Next morning, they tell each other what they have dreamed, but each still sticks to his or her own decision.

The Future – in the present
What will be the outcome of the mutiny? Each one experiences the mutiny for him or herself, and there is no need to stage it subsequently in action. A change in rhythm, through movement, and an alteration in tension.

On Shore
The group abandon their roles as the sailors, and become the families and friends of the men who have mutinied. They have received news of what has happened, and discuss both the past and the fate of the mutineers, and the effect on their own lives.

Past, Present and Future
Here, from a different standpoint, the group reflect on the work, and examine the consequences of what has taken place. The consummatory phase of the process carries forward into further experience.

In this example, the teacher has been largely responsible for the development of the work, operating with a consciousness of the formal principles of time and rhythm, but incorporating the offerings of the group in the development of the work. It is possible to identify moments in drama when the children begin to be consciously responsible for the direction of the work, and the purposes of the children and the teacher begin to move together. One example is of a group who, as American Indians, reject the idea of attacking the palefaces in favour of negotiation and alliance. These children were sufficiently experienced in the form to realise that the satisfactions of developing the work outweighed the satisfactions of immediate and violent action. They were working to postpone action.

An example of children developing a sense of time might be the following. A teacher was working with a group of infants, pretending to be the children of a village whose parents had not returned from work. After a night of waiting, the group set out in the snow to try to find their missing parents. Suddenly, a little girl pointed some way ahead, 'Look over there!' The teacher, realising that if the parents were discovered, the play was at an end, asked. 'What is it?' The child cautiously went ahead and picked something up. 'It's a hat.' Another child came forward and announced, 'It's like the hat my mother was wearing,' and the search continued. These children were working with a sense of time, of the future, but again in such a way as to postpone the climax of the work. By putting off the satisfaction of ending the search, they were strengthening the meaning of the work.

It may not always be the case that the teacher will have a sounder grasp than the children of the operation of formal elements within the work. It may be that the group will have an intuitive understanding of what will work best in a particular situation. A teacher was working with a group of children who had decided to be settlers attempting to make a new life in America. Their camp is visited by an American Indian, who promises to return and let them know his chief's decision about whether they may continue their journey across his territory. The children went on with the work of the camp, knowing that the next high moment of drama would be the return of the Indian. Then some of the group suggested that they should say their prayers and settle down for the night. Here was a recognition that there would be greater tension if the American Indians returned to a sleeping camp, than if he merely interrupted the bustle of the work. The camp settled down to sleep.

The teacher interrupted the drama at this point. She was unhappy about the fact that some of the group found it hard to settle down – their sleeping did not look convincing. She suggested that the group should merely sit up, in a thoughtful way, to await the American Indian's arrival. In spite of her advice, the class lay down to sleep once more. The American Indian (another teacher) entered the circle silently, placed a message from his chief in the centre, and withdrew. The sleeping settlers gradually awoke, and discovered the message in their midst. Here the first teacher was concerned with the external appearance of the work, and hoped that if these appearances were correct, they would enhance the work. The group, by their actions, showed a truer understanding of how tension operates in drama.

In educational drama, when both teacher and group have an understanding of the nature of the form in which they are working, there will be congruence and integrity in the make-believe. They will be working, not towards plot, but in a sense to suspend plot. Conflict will not arise because of external contriving, but will be embedded in situation and develop from the internal tensions of the work. Working as co-artists, forging the developing form and meaning of the work, they will create moments that are heavy with the weight of the past and great with things to come. But above all, the group will have found a genuine communal understanding, achieved an accepted group reality, and created the integrity and coherence of experience that is art.

Conclusion

I have attempted to show that the process of educational drama, like any other art, possesses form and functions through the operation of formal aesthetic elements. The activity of drama is far from being merely inchoate, exploratory and fragmented. When the process operates through the uniquely ordering features of time, tension and rhythm, it can become an experience that is unified, consummatory and aesthetic.

Awareness of the possibility of form within process is limited among drama teachers. Some teachers already have a conscious grasp of form within the process, and others, working intuitively as artists with their pupils, achieve the kind of dynamic organisation that gives form to the experience. Most drama teachers, however, see form as existing only in drama which develops towards theatre, and are not equipped by their training either to function as initiators of experience for their pupils or to control the unfolding creative process from within. Their teaching function is thus rendered largely ineffective.

Yet the responsibility of the teacher is clear. Only the teacher can help pupils to structure the experience of drama so that qualities of thinking and feeling are evoked which lead to intrinsic aesthetic learning. It is not enough to achieve cognitive content and instrumental learning through the work. Other school subjects can lead to learning of this kind. Instrumental learning can only be a part of education in the arts if it constantly relates in feeling and thought to the intrinsic aesthetic experience. Unless the learning that is achieved through drama is intrinsic to the subject, it is impossible to justify drama educationally.

When the process of educational drama is recognised as an art form, teachers will be likely to help their pupils to achieve the unique kind of knowing which can come from the experience of art. An understanding of the aesthetic nature of the process should assist teachers in initiating, structuring and evaluating drama experiences for their pupils. This understanding should lead to a recognition of the elements which drama and theatre share, and the essential ways in which they differ. Drama teachers working through this process need not feel that the experience they give their pupils is in any way less unified or satisfactory than work which leads to an end product. If teachers develop an awareness of the inner form of the process, they should begin to be able to structure the drama experience so that intrinsic aesthetic learning can take place.

The kind of aesthetic learning that occurs will depend on the unique meaning embodied in the work. Because of the special nature of drama, this meaning is likely to be concerned with human behaviour and its consequences. It is the task of the drama teacher to control the development of the work so that the pupils can experience, explore and reflect on that behaviour, its implications and consequences, from within the creative process that is drama. Unless the teacher is aware of the ordering aesthetic principles that operate in the process, he or she is faced with an extraordinarily difficult task.

I would not wish to argue for a sterile formalism or an effete aestheticism. The roots of art are in direct human experience. Experience arises from the interaction of people and their environment, and art celebrates that interaction with clarity and intensity. The participants in the drama process bring to it their own experience of the world. The drama teacher must build a bridge for the pupils between their experience and the meaning that is embodied in the drama. If the teacher fails, the work will be lacking in integrity and will be effective neither educationally nor aesthetically. In structuring the process according to aesthetic principles, the teacher is likely to achieve both educational and artistic objectives. The pupils will be able to make sense of their experience in the world and organise their experience in the drama process into the unity, coherence and significance of art.

Episode Two
Guidelines for Structuring Drama

Episode Two
Guidelines for Structuring Drama

We have seen from the chapters in Episode One that the aesthetic imperative which shapes drama educators' praxis is central to the kinds of activities that students encounter. In O'Neill's teaching, she is arguing for a grounded notion of artistic creation where all participants' life experiences are valued. Drawing on her knowledge of playwriting, dramaturgy and various theatrical traditions, she implicates her students in dramatic worlds where they have to interrogate and resolve problematic encounters. Being implicated might require pursuing an intriguing question, struggling with contradictions, working collaboratively and facing unforeseen events. Her major textbooks, *Drama Guidelines, Drama Structures, Drama Worlds* and *Dreamseekers* each contain accessible examples of how a teacher might learn to implicate students in imaginary worlds and accommodate their multiple and diverse responses.

Drama Guidelines, O'Neill's first significant foray into the world of publication, written with her past colleagues from the Inner London Education Authority, is a focussed introduction to many of the key themes which inform process drama. The title is significant in that it refers to principles which should inform teaching, not recipes that have to be transmitted. Most unsatisfying curricula can exist when teachers have their predetermined plan and know exactly where they are going before they start the journey. O'Neill has resisted this notion of the teacher being the sole owner of classroom learning. The Foreword to *Drama Guidelines* is indicative of this concern and highlights the need for teachers to be uncomfortable in their uncertainty, to work from the responses of the group and to constantly structure for ambiguity.

> Guide-lines are not guide-dogs. They are not intended to help along those who cannot see. Nor are they tram-lines, laid down to take the skill and

> adventure out of steering. Primarily guide-lines require us to ask the question 'Why?' and insist on staying for an answer.
>
> Reaching towards the truth, towards accurate perception of how things are or should be, is often as much a matter of questioning the answers as answering the questions. So I hope the ideas in these guide-lines will not be inertly received. They deserve to be widely discussed, reflected on and reacted to ... (Newman, in O'Neill *et al*, 1976)

There will be teachers whose only guideline is to remain in control of the lesson plan at every step. This is not only apparent in those whose principal concern is to deliver content, such as conventional instruction in theatre history and criticism, play production and analysis, technology and design, but we can also find teachers with a commitment to process drama being so much in ownership of the learning outcomes that there might as well be no students in the class. Thirty years on from the publication of *Drama Guidelines*, O'Neill still advocates for flexibility in planning. For instance, in The Recruiting Officer (see the Introduction), she began the process drama with clear direction and purpose.

> I want to get some spontaneity in our work. It's very hard for teachers to be spontaneous because they're constrained by curricula. Even with the arts. The arts suffer from having to deal with very structured curricula and very predictable outcomes. Now I know you have external pressures, these are part of all our work. But if there's no place for the unexpected, for the unpredictable, for the unknown even – then you're not, perhaps, going to learn as much than if you take a risk. So, just bear that in mind. When you work in the arts there has to be something unknown. If you control the whole experience, if you have everything structured within an inch of its life then you might just as well hand out the lesson plan and go have a cup of coffee. So, I'd like today, if I can, to see how good we are at thinking on our feet.

While the sessions in *Drama Guidelines* and the books which followed have specific objectives, O'Neill advocates a qualitative approach in education where aims can change, based on contextual circumstances. These sessions might focus on teaching theatre text and skills, curriculum content in language arts or social studies, and which endeavour to build the group's community health and interpersonal development. Each session has been practically adapted for a specific community. For example, a group of high school boys in their fifth year are studying *One day in the life of Ivan Denisovitch* by Alexander Solzhenitsyn; the objective is to probe the themes of the book without 'acting prison-camps' (O'Neill *et al*, 1976: 31-32). The teacher searches for non-conventional deprivations and has noted that that 'the normal hierarchy of the class is one of size and race.' She searches for a dramatic frame which enables the group to focus on two main ideas – deprivation and interdependence.

In a study of *Macbeth* with a class of fourth years, the objective of the lesson was to explore students' knowledge of the play, 'to reinforce that knowledge and motivate them to a further close study of the text' (O'Neill and Lambert, 1982: 219-222). Students create depictions, still images, of the vital incidents in Macbeth's career, they set up tribunals to inquire into Lady Macbeth's guilt, and imagine that Banquo has a wife who is just as ambitious for him as Lady Macbeth is for her husband.

In role as a talk show host, O'Neill endows the participants with the attitudes of famous people, not real celebrities but fictitious folk who have achieved fame. The teacher-in-role welcomes the guests to her studio and asks them two questions: What is the best thing about being famous? What is the worst thing? It is the latter question that changes the mood and the process drama is launched, exploring how public pressures can impact upon the private world (O'Neill, 1995: 104-10). The work becomes a powerful metaphor for how all people balance external expectations with their inner needs.

In a series of sessions exploring the African-American heritage, O'Neill and her colleagues work actively to enable students to engage with the curriculum where the aim is 'to foster a dialogic exchange, a conversation among different voices and traditions.' Students adopt a variety of roles and positions where they examine social injustice, explore the mistakes of the past and consider their hopes for a better future (Manley and O'Neill, 1997: ix, xv). This form of education is powered by problem posing encounters where students grapple with the devastating costs of prejudice, racism and overall human disenfranchisement.

These richly illuminative examples are structured around releasing the imagination and arousing students' capacity to commit to the curriculum. In the chapters which follow, we track the theoretical frameworks which inform the structuring of process drama. First, there is the requirement for teachers to understand that students are working in two domains: the fictional and the real. While drama is an imagined act, it is also a constructed one. 'It is happening to me,' might neatly describe the act of participation. Students in drama are exploring roles and relationships, they are experiencing enacted worlds in a supportive and protected environment.

Equally, though, they are aware they are creating an illusion: 'I am making it happen to me'. It is important that students can step out of the imaginary event so that they can clearly analyse the process. At the same time, teachers are conscious of pressing distancing devices into the drama. O'Neill is concerned with heightening the reflective stance of the class where her students can observe, examine, critique and contemplate their artistry. Participating at life's rate is seen as stifling the group's interpretive powers and lessening their ability to adeptly craft their dramatic play: 'I am making it happen: It is happening to me' could very well be the mantra of the process drama leader.

It will come as no surprise to readers familiar with O'Neill's praxis that one of the principal means through which students can achieve the dual stance of participant-observer is when the teacher goes into role. This teacher-in-role strategy is often misunderstood, but it is at the centre of the drama teacher's repertoire.

> The willingness of the teacher to centre and build the fictional world in this way is a powerful means of altering the atmosphere, relationships, and balance of power in the classroom, since it immediately extends the functions of the teacher within the lesson. In more traditional creative drama lessons, the teacher typically remains an external facilitator, a side coach, a director, or a 'loving ally', rather than working in role within the drama. 'Teacher-in-role' is closely identified with the distinguished drama educator, Dorothy Heathcote, who was the first to develop the strategy systematically. (O'Neill, 1997: 91)

These chapters describe the benefits of teacher-in-role and deconstruct the pedagogical functions served from within the drama as performer, director and playwright. Never the entertainer, the teacher-in-role can help build the group's commitment to and belief in the imaginary world. While some have argued that this stance can be too theatrical and manipulative, O'Neill reveals how the liminal stance of being *betwixt and between* can enable leaders-in-role to shatter stereotypes and hold participants accountable for their own learning. She argues that when educators work in role, they can:

- Launch the dramatic world quickly and economically
- Give status to the drama by being actively involved
- Invite immediate reactions from students by endowing them with roles that have the power to respond within the fictional situation
- Draw the group together in a purposeful enterprise
- Set relevant tasks for students

77

- Model appropriate language registers and behaviours
- Control and guide the development of the drama
- Present challenges that increase the tension
- Offer support and affirmation of students' roles. (O'Neill, 1997: 92-93)

Other strategies are referred to in this Episode including student role-play, mantle of the expert, tableaux and questioning. With each there is the assumption that the teacher will be an engaged professional who is able to share the process of learning with the group. 'It is not enough for the drama teacher to provide an initial stimulus, to throw a switch,' she claims, 'and then sit back and wait for the drama to happen' (O'Neill *et al*, 1976: 9). O'Neill activates the artistry of all those who experience process drama. She appeals for democratic, social and dialogical encounters where students are protected into emotion, and discover what is and is not possible as they strive toward the humane goals of liberation and freedom.

5

Imagined Worlds in Theatre
and Drama

This article first appeared in *Theory into Practice*, Volume XXIV, Number 3, Summer 1985. *Theory into Practice* is a journal of the College of Education, Ohio State University.

After several decades of a false and distorting polarisation, theatre and educational drama seem to be finding their true relationship. Teachers are becoming aware of the elements which drama and theatre share – elements which have long been recognised as the essential clay of the medium by the most effective theorists and practitioners. This article examines how the deeper purposes of drama and theatre can be mutually illuminating.

Drama as Social Encounter

When we watch a play in the theatre, we enter an imaginary world, a realm of illusion, created for us by the playwright, director, actors and everyone who has been involved in the production. They work together to present us with an 'imagined act' (Beckerman, 1970: 18). However realistically or naturalistically presented, we remain aware that we are watching a fiction, an illusion of actuality, a pretence.

This awareness lies at the heart of both theatre and drama. We may become deeply involved and absorbed, but 'disbelief is a necessary constant' (Elam, 1980: 108). The playwright selects for our attention some particular aspect of life or human behaviour from a context of expectations, and those who interpret the work present it for our scrutiny. Beckerman (1970) has called theatre a window through which we look at some aspects of life. We see through the illusion of action, which is presented to the actuality beyond.

As an audience, we may seem isolated from the action on stage, but we are engaging in a social encounter. Robinson (1983) has pointed out that theatre is an encounter, which takes place between actors and audience and refers to the relationship between them. As Elam (1980) shows, it is the spectators who initiate the theatrical communicative process. Their apparent passivity is an active choice. Without the engagement of the audience there is no relationship, no communication and no theatre. An audience works hard to make sense of the scattered bits of dramatic information it receives. From the moment the play begins we speculate, make assumptions and develop expectations about the world unfolding before us. 'The spectator translates what he sees and hears on the stage into a fictional dramatic world characterised by a set of physical properties, a set of agents, and a course of time-bound events' (Elam, 1980: 98).

The construction of this dramatic world, the realm of illusion, is at least partly our own creation, the result of our efforts to piece together a dramatic content whose expression is fragmented and incomplete. The details of this world emerge gradually, are subject to change and are not fully known until the drama is over. We read the clues we receive from the people in the play and their actions and statements. The specifications of the fictional world are revealed gradually from within through references given by the individuals who inhabit it. The dramatic world defines itself rather than being set up from outside.

In educational drama, we are also struggling to make sense of a dramatic representation which is, by its nature, 'non-linear, discontinuous, and incomplete' (Elam, 1980: 99). In both theatre and drama we try to piece together what we perceive to be the underlying logic of the action. We supplement the hypothetical world we are witnessing on stage or creating in the classroom with our own knowledge and experience of the real world, measuring the fictional against the actual.

At a play, our knowledge and experience of the conventions of theatre assist us. Our expectations are guided by what we know of the author, what we may have read or heard about the production, and even by the title. Similar expectations apply in educational drama. The previous experience of the class in drama, familiarity with the teacher's way of working, and the chosen subject matter of the lesson provide clues about some of the features the fictional world may contain.

For example, children who want to do a story about the Three Little Pigs may anticipate that their imaginary world will contain houses for the pigs, small but brave and resourceful pigs, and a large and wicked wolf. They will also know that despite the wolf's efforts the little pigs will triumph. Teenagers asked to construct a drama about bank robberies or Dracula are also likely to have clear expectations about some of the elements the drama may contain, and these expectations will assist them in finding roles, language and action appropriate to that world. Such expectations may produce stereotyped responses at first, but these are likely to fade as the work grows in complexity. Rules of behaviour are partly anticipated and partly forged in process.

The theatregoer learns the rules of the game largely through experience, not just of theatre, but also of play, games and other representations. The same is true of the child taking part in a drama lesson. Where either the kind of theatrical representation being viewed or the activity in the drama lesson is unfamiliar, there will be an attempt to decode what has happened, to grasp the rules of an unfamiliar game. Much of the enjoyment which arises from drama comes from the effort to discover its underlying principles. To pay this kind of close attention implies cognition, motivation, and emotion (Beckerman, 1970). Our attention is arrested, we react with empathy and heightened awareness, and our imagination is concentrated and structured by what we experience.

Drama as Self-Transcendence

Why should it seem pleasurable and worthwhile to make this kind of concentrated effort – an effort on which the success of every piece of theatre or drama depends? Koestler (1975) describes a need to transcend the narrow confines of our personal identity and participate in other forms of existence. He claims there is intrinsic value in illusion. This value derives from the transfer of our attention to a plane remote from self-interest. The removal of interest, attention, and emotion to a different time and location is an act of self-transcendence. Although all art contains the possibility of taking us beyond ourselves, theatre and drama demand actual participation in an illusion, which inhibits self-assertive tendencies and facilitates self-transcending tendencies. Cassirer (1944) asserts that art turns emotion into a means of self-liberation and gives us inner freedom.

The educational value of drama lies in the promotion of these self-transcending tendencies. Bolton (1984) uses the term distortion to describe earlier claims for drama as a vehicle for individual growth. He expresses the notion of self-transcendence by saying that drama is never about oneself, but is always concerned with something outside oneself. It is a social and not a solitary experience. The essential nature of the dramatic medium is a liberating act of imagination, a dual consciousness in which the real and fictional worlds are held together in the mind.

Creating Dramatic Context

The pretence of theatre and the dual awareness with which we receive and respond to that pretence are central to educational drama, and the creation of an imaginary world, a dramatic context for the action, is primary. Drama lessons which rely on games and exercises to the neglect of the creation of a dramatic context are avoiding the essential activity of drama – the construction of a realm of illusion. Bolton (1984) identifies the influence of Brian Way as significant in the growth of the kind of work which avoids the creation of dramatic context – the very essence of the medium.

A group of children engaged in make-believe play may be closer to a fictional world and thus nearer to the true life of the theatre than actors practicing concentration or improvisational exercises. Cassirer (1944) distinguishes between play and art by noting three kinds of imagination – the power of invention, the power of personification and the power to produce pure, sensuous forms. Play, he claims, uses the first two powers of imagination but not the last. Play rearranges and redistributes our materials, while art is constructive and creative in another sense. Play transforms objects, but art is 'the discovery of a new world' (p164).

Several commentators have noted the connections between make-believe play and educational drama and have used the work of play theorists to explain and support their explications of the drama activity. As in play, in drama we may be merely rearranging our materials but, because of the nature of the activity and the possibility it carries of the growth of a dramatic world, drama also has a formative aspect. The teacher may be actively working with aesthetic intention, and formal aesthetic elements will help to shape the development of the work (O'Neill, 1978).

For Cassirer (1944), the boundary between play and art is a conscious and reflective attitude. In drama, action may appear to be paramount and reflection may be held to a minimum (Moffett, 1968) but, for many practitioners, reflection is a crucial element. In drama we experience an 'as if' world and at the same time create the means of reflecting on existence (Heathcote, 1978). A conscious and reflective attitude is likely to develop in drama because of the dynamic relationship between reality and pretence. In the theatre, the spectators are caught up in a complex pattern of expectation and response. Although they agree to be engrossed by the illusion being created, they do not enter it. The isolation of the events on the stage and the lines of demarcation between actors and audience are an essential part of the interaction. There may be a relationship between actors and audience, but the actors are using what Bolton (1984: 128) calls 'a one-way communication pattern.'

The drama lesson has no such barriers. Communication is between participants who are free to negotiate meaning. They are the agents of the drama. The protective distance between actors and audience, both actual and virtual, vanishes in the drama lesson, making it important that the teacher provide another kind of distancing for pupils, to 'protect them into emotion' (Bolton, 1984). One kind of distancing device is Heathcote's use of 'mantle of the expert' (Johnson and O'Neill, 1984).

Because participants in a drama lesson are caught up in the here and now of what is happening, more complex demands are made on them than on a theatre audience. While they usually lack the support to their make-believe provided in the theatre – script, sets, costumes, lighting, etc. – such supports are not a necessity. Pupils may rapidly select objects and materials which they transform in use to assist them in creating their world of illusion, or they may rearrange the space and furniture available to correspond with what they perceive as some of the necessary features of the drama setting.

The Drama Setting

If the teacher knows in advance the context of the drama, it may be possible to plan the early stages of the work so that the dramatic world comes more easily into being. It is wise to consider the best use of available space and furniture. To remain seated at desks may be appropriate for a press conference but unsuitable for a tribunal or secret gang meeting. Some classes may prefer to make decisions about the environment themselves, others may respond to the surprise of entering a classroom which has been transformed.

Teachers who have access to a drama studio may be able to create quite powerful effects. But too much effort to establish an elaborate setting for the drama lesson may not only predetermine outcomes and reduce the possibility of negotiation but actually hinder the creation of the dramatic world. Even the most elaborate stage design only suggests a domain which does not coincide with its actual physical limits (Elam, 1980). It is a mental construct on the part of the spectator.

If the drama is over-resourced, less effort is required of the participants in decoding the situation, and the use of their powers of invention and transformation will be limited. The dramatic world of educational drama is most valuable both educationally and aesthetically when its construction is shared and its meaning negotiated. As the work progresses, pupils may find it necessary to bring in objects or costumes, but these should be enrichments of the work and not mere elaboration. At no point should these items become, as may easily happen, more important than the meaning being generated. In the same way, symbolic objects are difficult to select at the beginning of the work, but may emerge from it.

Working in Role

One of the most effective and economical ways of setting the dramatic world in motion is for the teacher to work in role. The role shares some of the qualities of a stage presentation in that it is there to be looked at – it uses 'sign' (Heathcote, 1982). Its actions, gestures, and words can be read by the class. It is a presentation, not a performance, and should excite the kind of attention from the participants that will cause them to search for clues about the features of the fictional world being created. One of the clues they will be searching for is a sense of their own relationship to the role – their own role function – and their power in relationship to the role. Although many aspects of the context may already have been mutually agreed upon (e.g. subject matter, starting point, roles of class and teacher) the growth of the dramatic world may contain surprising and unpredictable elements.

The keys to the world being constructed lie primarily in the roles participants adopt or are given and in what they say. They are the agents of what is taking place, the 'makers of the future' (Langer, 1953: 306). Participants may discover responses in themselves which are unexpected and find, through their roles and the challenge of the fictional situation, skills and capacities of which they were unaware. Like the actors in a play, participants in drama construct the dramatic world and reveal it through their actions and statements. The characteristics of the dramatic world are gradually revealed, as are the identities of its inhabitants, their histories and characteristics. The actors in both drama and theatre are 'leaning into the future' (Beckerman, 1970: 148). They are in the process of 'becoming.'

The successful creation of an imagined world depends to a considerable extent on the degree to which participants can make links between the world of illusion and their understanding of the real world. They will not be attempting a mere imitation of real life. Rather, like children at play, they will be rearranging and transforming the components of the world they know in actuality into, at the least, fresh patterns and, at best, the kind of abstraction and generalisation which approaches art. For them, the value of this abstraction may be to reduce reality to manageable proportions.

One of the determinants of whether the work has achieved aesthetic significance is the quality of the dramatic experience. But even if the product – the meaning which is negotiated and the world which is created – is less than excellent, the creation of illusion is still of value (Koestler, 1975). It enables participants to transcend the narrow confines of their personal identity and allows them to participate in other forms of existence.

A Drama Session

A recent drama session illustrates the way in which a fictional world can grow. The class was a mixed group of 14-year-olds in an inner London comprehensive school. In their drama lessons they were accustomed to using games and exercises and making up scenes. Developing an idea throughout a two-hour session and working in role were less familiar to them.

The lesson took place during the commemoration of the 40th anniversary of the invasion of France by the Allied Forces. I discussed with the class the idea that, in drama, one can play the game of 'What if...?', looking at events in history and examining what might have happened if they had turned out differently. The class agreed to explore what life might have been like for them if Germany had successfully invaded England in 1940. In the following description, the **text in bold** (left-hand column) recounts the events of the lesson, while the *text in italic* (right-hand column) describes features of the fictional world as they developed and emphasises teaching points.

EPISODE 1

We created newspaper headlines, which might have appeared at the time to chart the progress of the invasion. I suggested that we write these as if they came from three different phases of the invasion: (a) the landings of the German army when headlines would be designed to boost morale, hide the extent of the invasion and strengthen resistance; (b) armed resistance to the invaders; and (c) the final phase of occupation with newspapers and other media in the hands of the German propagandists. After some initial hesitation, they handled the task competently. As they created the headlines, I wrote them on the blackboard. Our drama would begin, I said, at the point when the country had been largely stabilised.

It was important for the class to begin to conceptualise the changed nature of the world we were creating. They had to create a complex series of events and feel the difference between an England that was eventually victorious and one which was defeated, occupied and isolated. Factual details emerged from these headlines, such as the flight of the Royal Family to Canada, the disappearance of Churchill, and the overthrow of the army. This was an intellectual task, outside any dramatic context and yet creating it. Working on the headlines as a group, the class created the notion of German dominance and British submission. If I merely told them this was the case, they might have rejected it. This initial task protected them into the drama, but it then became essential to find some direct link with their own experience. The effect on their schooling seemed a useful link and provided an area in which they were experts.

EPISODE 2

In the next phase of the lesson, I worked in role. I asked the class to imagine that they were all young people at school, but several years older than their real ages – perhaps 17 or 18. Their school had been closed during the invasion but, now that peace and order had been established, it had re-opened. After discussion, the class decided they would be waiting in their sixth-form common room for lessons to begin. I entered in role and introduced myself as Miss Smith. I explained that I was replacing their previous teacher, Miss Wilson, and would be their new teacher. They would have to realise that there would be some changes, but if they were sensible and realistic they would soon agree that it was best to accept these changes and apply themselves to their work. Their response was very guarded, but obviously hostile and suspicious. They questioned me closely about my background and experience, and the whereabouts of their previous teacher, Miss Wilson. One boy challenged me directly and accused me of being a German spy. I assured him that I was as English as he was and begged him to be careful of what he said. Since we couldn't do anything directly to resist the Germans, who were now in charge, it was sensible to try to work with them for the safety and stability of the country.

In our fictional world, the invasion caused an upheaval in society, but there was now sufficient stability for schools to re-open. Making them older than their real selves gave them greater responsibility and more choices. Although some aspects remained familiar, this was clearly a world of implied danger where it was unwise to resist or oppose even unwelcome changes. In this world, it was difficult to know whom to trust. Authority figures appeared rather differently and a different kind of power lay behind them. People, Miss Wilson for example, may disappear suddenly and without reason. It was dangerous to reveal one's true feelings. I tried to avoid providing any direct answers and thus building too many details of the fictional world myself. My unease and evasiveness fitted the role I was playing. I also tried to avoid encouraging stereotyped responses. This phase of the lesson was brief and some of the details which had emerged were clarified in discussion afterwards. I asked the class to comment on their view of the role I was playing, which provided the only concrete evidence of the new regime and its nature. Some saw Miss Smith as shifty, lying and evasive. One girl said she'd seen a person who was afraid.

EPISODE 3

I asked each pupil to mention one way in which his or her school had altered under the new regime. The changes they mentioned included staff, particularly the senior teachers, compulsory identity cards and passes, prominently displayed portraits of Hitler, German hymns and music at school assembly, and alterations in the school curriculum. In particular, they mentioned changes in the teaching of history and the introduction of compulsory German.

It was important not to impose my ideas of change on the class. It would have been easy, using the role of Miss Smith, to announce a number of changes and demand acceptance from the pupils. But a more interesting and complex world would develop if they invented and accepted changes which demonstrated their impotence and subordination. This task took place outside the dramatic context.

EPISODE 4

We discussed how the pupils might feel about the changes taking place in their school. Would they accept them, or would some people show their dislike of what was happening? It was suggested that anti-German slogans might appear. Working in small groups, the pupils invented graffiti which they wrote on large pieces of paper -'V' for victory, 'Nazis out', and various slogans calling for resistance.

The tension of possible resistance was introduced. The existence of the graffiti confirmed that some of the pupils were prepared to make some kind of stand against the authorities. Resistance had become a feature of our world and it was created by the class. It was not the action-packed, cliché resistance of a war movie, but the kind that was credible within a school context.

EPISODE 5

As Miss Smith, I called the class together again, and explained that the appearance of foolish and wicked graffiti in school had created a problem for the school authorities. I knew that none of them could be responsible for this vandalism, and they were quick to agree that they'd had nothing to do with it. However, I said I was sure that they knew the names of those responsible. It would be very sensible of them and show their maturity if they were careful not to encourage or associate with such foolish young people. They might, after all, be judged by their friends. By giving me the names of these misguided young people, they would enable me to have a quiet word with them and warn them of the possibly serious consequences of such activity. The students insisted they knew nothing about it, but promised to tell me if they heard anything. Suddenly, I changed direction, and asked them if they knew the whereabouts of David. I knew he was a member of the class, but he hadn't attended school for several weeks. Had any of them seen him? The school authorities were worried about him and anxious to find him. In their responses to these questions, many new details began to emerge. David was a close friend of one of the boys and the boyfriend of one of the girls. These pupils volunteered this information. His parents had been shot shortly after the invasion. David was no longer living at home, and his elder brother had been in the resistance movement. It was clear that David was also involved. I left them with a warning that things wouldn't stop there. The principal may want to question them about their knowledge of David. They'd be wise to co-operate.

Now our world acquired a sinister new perspective – it was a place in which one may be asked to betray one's friends. Again, the basis of the situation may have been familiar to them – not giving away a wrongdoer's name to the authorities – but the consequences in our fictional world, although disguised, were likely to be more dangerous. In this section of the work, the reaction of the class to Miss Smith was much more subtle than in the first meeting. The students were learning the game of negotiating in role and were moving to more thoughtful and complex responses. A new element was introduced and accepted without question by the class. From this point, they had the confidence to start creating details of our world within the drama itself. They listened intently and constructed details which were appropriate to previous contributions. The notion of resistance to the Germans was now embodied in a boy of their own age, whom they created together. His characteristics and previous history emerged. Collaboration and betrayal now had a more concrete meaning. By their contributions in this part of the work particularly they showed their belief in and commitment to the drama.

87

EPISODE 6

I asked for a volunteer to take on the role of Mr. Muller, the school principal. One boy agreed. He must conduct an interrogation of the boy and girl who have admitted to knowing David well. The rest of the class listened in on the interrogation, and I suggested that, if they wanted to, they could freeze the action and advise those playing the scene on what they should say or how they should behave. The class watched the scene with considerable involvement and made several useful suggestions. The two friends were adept at protesting their innocence and ignorance, and the boy who took on the role of principal avoided any Nazi clichés, although he was a more overtly threatening figure than Miss Smith.

Here, the people involved in the scene were working with a sense of theatre, but were protected by the involvement of the rest of the group and the possibility of freezing the action – a convention which allowed for input and reflection by the rest of the class. The boy who took the role of principal worked with a considerable sense of authority – an authority which was not just personal, but which was supported by the power of the regime.

EPISODE 7

I asked the class to work in pairs, one remaining a pupil of the school and the other taking the role of one of their parents. The parents had been told that their son or daughter might be selected to attend an International Youth Congress in Vienna, to celebrate the stabilisation and unification of Europe under National Socialism. This would be a wonderful opportunity for their child, with implications for future jobs or university chances. The only thing that might prevent their child's selection was the fact that he or she was not being very co-operative and persisted in protecting undesirable friends. The parents were asked to put pressure on their children to co-operate with the authorities.

In this part of the work many new details emerged. These included parental attitudes towards their children, their ambitions for them and their relationships with them. Attitudes to the occupation also varied. Some parents urged their children to play safe and conform while others encouraged resistance and independence. There was a growing sense of the world outside – a Europe united and pacified under Hitler, as well as a broader sense of the world of home and school.

EPISODE 8

The class worked in small groups, preparing and showing a situation which I suggested. The scene was a youth club where David, who had been wounded while attempting sabotage, sought refuge. Each scene showed how David was received – whether his friends took the risk of hiding him and whether they felt they could trust each other. Some, who were eager to be selected for the Youth Congress, seemed rather untrustworthy.

This was a theatre activity to be briefly rehearsed and performed. It was watched, not for entertainment or to display or enjoy theatrical skills, but for the further information it might contain. Pupils were sufficiently confident to display a range of possible reactions; not just stereotyped heroism but a sense of loyalty and friendship with an awareness of what the consequences of that loyalty might be.

EPISODE 9

As a last activity in this long session, I asked the class to prepare two radio broadcasts, one from the resistance underground radio station and the other from the BBC giving the official German news. This task echoed the headlines with which we had begun the session and showed the contrast between the two views of the dramatic world we had created.

Although we would not finish the drama in this session, a sense of completion was needed. This activity also had a reflective purpose and summed up what had gone before.

The class continued to work on this theme in subsequent lessons which included attempts to persuade other young people to resist, attempts at sabotage, retraining by the authorities, the use of propaganda and other characteristics of the fictional world which had interested them. From this work they achieved a sense of discovery, an awareness of their own capacities, and a feeling of growing effectiveness both personally and in the drama. They succeeded in creating a world which, although fictional, possessed an inner logic. The roles they adopted were close to their own roles in real life but allowed them, within the safety of the pretence, to experience the challenge of oppression, of having their loyalty tested, of defining friendship and of finding within themselves both courage and resourcefulness.

Bruner (1960) has called our society an 'entertainment-oriented, mass communication culture, where spectatorship and passivity are dangers.' He regards techniques of arousing attention in school as being the first steps towards establishing 'an active autonomy of attention that is the antithesis of the spectator's passivity.' Perhaps the greatest educational value of the session described above is that for two hours the class maintained the delicate balance of a dual consciousness and focused its attention and empathy on an illusory but possible world. This world was the creation and responsibility of the group members, who simultaneously constructed and decoded the activity. In drama as in the theatre, the individual participants or spectators must make sense of what is happening. The final responsibility for the meaning of what is constructed is theirs.

6
Transforming Texts: Intelligences in Action

Originally appeared in *English Journal*, 84 (Dec, 1995) co-authored with T. Rogers and J. Jasinski

A group of ninth grade students is responding to the task of creating a tableau or still picture of a scene from *To Kill a Mockingbird* by Harper Lee. To create a tableau, the students use their own bodies to represent a significant moment in the story. As they work together, they negotiate decisions, comment on key scenes in the book, gesture, sing, argue, joke, imagine and finally create their tableau that they share with the rest of the class.

S: We could, we could un...

S: We could do the fire.

S: No, that's kind of boring.

S: Atticus in front of the jail?

S: That's not a high point...

S: The fire would take four people... what?

S: How many people?

S: We could do the church – when they go to church with Calpurnia.

S: And do what? Sing? Ah ... ah... (singing)

S: I think the fire. We could be passing buckets and...

S: That's a good idea. So maybe one of you could be the house.

S: I'll be the house, I wanna burn...

S: I wanna burn because I didn't read the book and I don't want to be passing the water...

S: I read the book so I deserve to burn...

S: We could both burn...

S: Yea, you could make the house like this (gestures). Yeah, we're gonna burn...

T: OK, let's look at this tableau. Let's look at what they've done. Ah, that's clever. This is so different. What's different about it?

S: Um, she's at the house. She's helping put out the fire. Kinda like the whole community helping out.

T: Yes, the whole community is helping out, there's a kind of a chain with the buckets of water. And there's action. They're actually trying to prevent the fire. In the other tableau they were just standing around. Very good. I like the house. That's an interesting way to use people in your group.

In creating and presenting their tableau, the students draw on a range of abilities or 'intelligences' (Gardner, 1983). They have moved, visualised and verbally negotiated in order to develop a shared-interpretation of a key event in the novel. In addition, they have been rewarded for this work in a literature class, which might otherwise be filled only with tired question-answer routines. Process drama breaks away from these patterns of responding to literature and elicits more engaged and dynamic interpretations. In this article we illustrate the use of drama as a form of literary response. We suggest that drama allows students to develop and exhibit a range of skills and to demonstrate their literary understandings in 'unschooled' ways (Gardner, 1991). Once demonstrated, these understandings can be the building blocks of new, more powerful ways of knowing.

Drama as a Response to Literature

Since literary works themselves are indeterminate (e.g. Iser, 1978), the exploration of the possibilities of a story's meanings may be best accomplished through ongoing dialogue, movement, and play rather than through static interpretations. Literary texts are never final. As Bakhtin noted, they are filled with ambivalence, conflict, multivocality, and remain open to transformation (Stewart, 1981). Using drama to express literary meanings through a variety of modes of expression allows the interpretative process to be equally fluid, changing and transformative. Both literature and drama invite students to enter, experience and explore imagined worlds. By responding through drama, students are encouraged to move away from normal classroom activities into the creation of new, imagined contexts that draw on the reader's secondary worlds (Benton, 1992) and allow these worlds to be examined and understood in immediate and concrete ways. When drama is used to encounter a particular text, the range of competencies in which students function is greatly enlarged as they interrogate, represent, transform and interpret the emerging meaning. In order to take part, students are required to draw on their understandings of human behaviour, on their practical knowledge of themselves and others, and on their aesthetic and imaginative sensibilities (Eisner, 1985b).

The parameters of the drama are defined by the text, in this case Harper Lee's *To Kill a Mockingbird*, but the students also bring their own abilities, experiences and insights to the task of exploring, developing and articulating an imagined world where text and drama mingle and interpenetrate. Drama fosters the retelling, extension, elaboration or enactment of events in the original text, as well as the exploration of individual characters' motives and behaviour. Students create multiple worlds and possibilities of meaning not only through word but also through gesture, visualisation, and movement (Rogers and O'Neill, 1993; O'Neill and Rogers, 1994).

Tableaux

The tableau or freeze frame used in the example at the beginning of this article is an effective drama technique that can be used with almost any literary text. An image of some key moment from the text is prepared by students working in small groups and shared with the rest of the class. This is a safe and purposeful task. In devising these images, the students use their own bodies to create a significant moment in the story, an abstract idea or a mental state. The students become physically involved but the technique does not demand any great theatrical skill. The images that are created may be naturalistic, such as pictures for an illustrated edition of *To Kill a Mockingbird*, or more abstract, such as an image of Justice as Atticus might imagine it. In composing these images, students are using their knowledge and understanding of the text to engage in a highly selective, economical and controlled form of expression which is available to be read and interpreted by the rest of the class.

Drawing on abilities related to movement, visualisation and interaction with space, tableaux can be used to discover and display what the students already know about a topic or theme; to develop a chronology of significant moments in the story; or to predict different outcomes. The significance of the use of the tableau in the classroom lies in its expansion of the students' capacity to perceive. It invites the observers to interrogate it for possible meanings, and both information and insight can be shaped and shared. However, the use of tableaux will not automatically result in reflection, interpretation or elaboration. Without the teacher's encouragement and questioning, and the deliberate adoption of an interpretive stance, the task will not necessarily modify or extend students' thinking.

Role-play

Following the tableaux, the students in this class are asked to become citizens of the town of Maycomb. The teacher takes on the role of a social worker who visits the Cunningham family, one of the poor but righteous families in the community.

T: (Out of role) Can you imagine that you are townspeople? And can I introduce myself? ... (In role) I'm from Children's Welfare Society and I'm told there are a number of families in this town who are having trouble with their children. Is that right?

Ss: Yes, yes.

T: Now I've been given some names. I don't know which you think is the most important family for me to see – the most urgent case – because I think some of these kids need the help of my Society. Who do you think I should see?

Ss: The Cunninghams.

T: The Cunninghams? Would you like to tell me what difficulties they have? I think I have them on my list (looks at list). Yes.

Ss: They're a poor family.

T: Very poor?

Ss: Yeah. They can't afford to pay people with money so they pay with crops and produce.

T: So are they really kind of no-good?

S: No, they're kind people, and they'll always repay you, but they just – it will take them time.

T: Well, our Society has some funds, and I'll go and visit them and give them some funds, to help them.

S: Well, the Cunninghams won't take it.

T: (Out of role) Let's see if they would... OK, I'm gonna knock on their door and see if they take some charity from me ... (to other students). You can give them advice.

Here the teacher, in role, is raising possibilities and inviting the students as townspeople to predict and advise, which involves adopting several perspectives, those of participant and those of more detached consultants. The students, with little prior experience with dramatic activities, fill these roles easily and insightfully:

T: ... um, oh, good morning Mr. and Mrs. Cunningham. I'm from the Children's Welfare Society, and I understand you've been having problems lately: Is that right?

S: (as Mrs. Cunningham) No. No. We all get along fine.

T: Well, but ah, I know that you do, and I can see that you manage very well. Your place is very neat and tidy and don't you keep the children clean. (lowers voice) I understand that your children, well, go to school hungry, is that right? (Cunninghams shake their heads) No?

Other Ss: Yeah, fight back.

T: Oh, now come along. I know that you do your best for them, but my information is that people say that you can't afford to feed your children.

T: (out of role to the other students) What do you think they will say to that?

Other Ss: Liar! Fight back!

T: (out of role) They're going to get mad? (Turns back to Cunninghams) Now look, I've got some money here and I can give you enough to provide lunches for your children.

S: (as Mrs. C) We really cannot accept your money.

T: Why not?

S: (as Mrs. C) We have our pride.

T: You have your pride? Well pride isn't going to fill your children's stomachs.

(Ss give conflicting advice to Cunninghams, both to get mad and to take the money.)

S: (as Mrs. C) We don't want your help. Go see the Ewells.

T: Now wouldn't you sooner, now don't feel angry, now take this money from me.

S: I wouldn't be able to pay it back.

T: Well, I don't want it paid back. It's a – gift. It's charity.

S: We don't want your charity.

T: Don't want my charity? That's fine. I'll go somewhere else where I'm appreciated.

In this example of dramatic role-play, the students are called upon to grasp the perspectives of the characters in the story and to act upon those understandings in empathetic and insightful ways. To do this, they draw on their intrapersonal intelligence; that is, on their knowledge of themselves and of feelings of pride, of shame and of anger. For instance, at the moment that Mrs. Cunningham admits she would not be able to pay back the money, the student in that role is drawing on her knowledge of the Cunningham family, her understanding of pride and her unfolding sense of the tension in the dramatic moment. That tension arises from the conflicting stances of the participants, the Cunninghams and the social worker and their very different views of how one lives in the world, as well as from advice coming from the other students as their consultants. Here students draw also on their interpersonal intelligence, or knowledge and awareness of others. All this takes place in a linguistic and social context that is being created and negotiated by students and teachers. In short, the students are drawing on a range of intelligences to create meanings across the worlds of the drama, the reader(s) and the literary text itself.

Teacher-in-Role

Drama makes demands on the teacher as well as on the students, particularly when the teacher takes on a role in the drama. The benefits for the teacher of working in role include the possibility of initiating the drama economically, creating atmosphere, modelling appropriate behaviour and language, supporting the students' efforts, and challenging the students' familiar responses (O'Neill and Lambert, 1982). No acting skills are necessary. Often the most effective roles are those that seem close to the teacher's regular function – chairing a meeting, asking questions, discussing the pros and cons of an event. The difference is that the role will always have an attitude to the event, seeking information, persuading, patronising, opposing or, in this case, offering charity. The teacher-in-role does not just demonstrate or act and is never merely an extra, one of the crowd 'adding to the number in the cast' (Johnson and O'Neill, 1984). His or her function is very different.

It is important to note that when the teacher takes on a role, the power relationships in the classroom are altered. In this example, the students are free to encourage Mrs. Cunningham in her opposition to the teacher-in-role as a social worker, and they take advantage of this implicit freedom without stepping outside the range of appropriate responses. The teacher is not trapped in her role but steps in and out of the drama when she needs input or advice from the students.

In the next example, the responses of the mean Ewells to the social worker require a transfer of authority from teacher to students. One example of this exchange of power is the reliance of the teacher-in-role on the advice of the students:

S: Let me be Mr. Ewell.

T: Okay, there's Mr. Ewell.

S: I want to be Mr. Ewell.

T: You're one of the kids. All of you are the Ewell kids (pointing to a small group of students). There's a whole bunch of them. They're mean and dirty.

S: I'll be mean.

T: OK. Here I go. (out of role, turns to the rest of the class) What advice would you give me?

S: Be aggressive.

T: Aggressive?

S: They're going to be aggressive right back so you can't be this quiet little person.

Here, the teacher's role-play is modified by the students' suggestions. They display a grasp of character and situation in the advice they give.

T: Well, I'll be ... this is one of the dirtiest farms I've been on. The whole place is filthy. OK. (knocks on 'door') Good morning. Mr. Ewell, is he here?

S: (as Ewell child) Yes. Wait.

S: (as Mr. Ewell) Right here (extends hand).

T: (begins to take hand and then pulls away) Oh, there you are. Oh, I'm very glad to meet you. I understand you have quite a large family.

The student as Mr. Ewell endows the other students with roles and names, which they readily accept and begin to elaborate on.

S: (as Mr. Ewell) This is Joey (hand on boy's shoulder). Little Bob (hand on other boy's shoulder).

T: Fine boys. Why aren't they in school?

S: (as a boy) We don't have to go to school.

S: (as Mr. Ewell) I teach them plenty right here.

T: I'm sorry, but I have to tell you that there is a law that requires your children to attend school. I understand that little Bob is in the... what... first grade?

S: He's been in there a couple of years.

T: So I understand, but I mean, shouldn't you send your children to school? He doesn't go often enough.

S: (as a boy) We don't wanna go.

S: (as another child) Yeah.

T: I'm talking to your father, do you mind?

(laughter)

Next, the teacher endows one of the students with a specific role in the family and begins to challenge her within that role.

T: (to another student) Um, you're the oldest girl in the family, is that right?

S: Yeah.

T: You look after the others. Couldn't you get them a little cleaner? And they seem to be rather badly dressed.

S: (as the older girl) I'm badly dressed?

T: Um, you look very nice my dear, but the younger children seem a little...

S: Well, I like the way l look.

S: We don't care.

S: (as Mr. Ewell) They're clean.

T: They're clean? Um, can't you control your children, Mr. Ewell?

S: No.

S: Be quiet, Dad!

The teacher picks up on this inappropriate challenge to Mr. Ewell's authority and deals with it out of role, not by denying it but by seeking the opinions of the other students.

T: (out of role to rest of class) Do you think he'd get away with that?

S: (as Mr. Ewell, but out of role) No, I'd take him by the ear and hold him right there.

S: He'd get beat.

T: (out of role) I think he would hit him... because these kids wouldn't get away with it. I might need to see that you were a bit afraid of your dad, because she's certainly afraid of her dad, isn't she? (in role) Urn, Mr. Ewell will you please make sure your children get to school?

S: (as Mr. Ewell) Um, I work in the day so...

S: I don't wanna go! We need to help pa in the fields.

S: (as Mr. Ewell) I can't really be sure they get to school. Plus they don't enforce the law. They don't come looking for me so...

T: Well, I'm afraid I going to have to report this to the authorities because they ought to be in school. School one day a year is not enough to get out of this dump you live in ...

S: We're doing fine. We need to help our dad out in the fields...

S: (as Mr. Ewell) Well, I have my own business...

S: (as older sister) How would they pay for their lunches?

T: I'm prepared to give you some money: How about that?

S: (as Mr. Ewell) I'll take it.

T: (out of role) What do you think he does with the money?

Ss: He spends it on himself ... He'll never give it back ... He buys some booze ...

T: He's gonna buy some moonshine...

Later, these students went on to write in role as the characters in the novel, and their writing was informed by the active understanding of character that the drama had encouraged.

Intelligences in Action

As these examples demonstrate, drama can promote an interactive and dynamic kind of classroom participation. Tired interaction patterns are replaced with lively and engaging dialogues, and students are empowered to question, challenge, interpret and reflect on the themes of literary works. They are allowed to learn and to display these learnings in multiple and distinctive ways (Gardner, 1991). Gardner's work helps us to see that, in many classrooms, students are not developing rich understandings because they are limited to traditional forms of linguistic interaction. When interactions and intelligences are supported by more open contexts of learning such as drama, students reveal abilities and understandings that surprise both their teachers and themselves.

As Wayne Booth noted in his classic book, *The Rhetoric of Fiction* (1961), 'In any reading experience there is an implied dialogue among author, narrator, the other characters and the reader' (p155). Drama expands this dialogue and makes it immediate and concrete as well as (paradoxically) imagined. The simultaneous presence of the real and the fictional in drama encourages multiple and creative forms of expression and frames of mind not commonly found in classrooms.

7

Dialogue and Drama

Originally published as 'Dialogue and Drama: Transformation of Events, Ideas, and Teachers' in *Language Arts* (1989), 66 (2): 147-59.

> Dialogue is a moment when humans meet to reflect on their reality as they make it and remake it. (Shor and Freire, 1987: 98)

If we are to establish dialogue in our classrooms that is truly creative and reflective, we must consider the context in which this dialogue is embedded, its content, and the kinds of relationships which will make it live.

Of the many teaching strategies which are likely to promote dialogue, the approach which has the greatest potential and yet is the least often used is drama in education – where teacher and students co-create fictional roles and contexts in order to explore and reflect on some issue, concept, relationship or event. This kind of drama is a complex, many-faceted process and a shared learning experience. The process has little in common with the kind of creative dramatics that may focus on individual pantomimes, skills training, the re-enactment of a story or the presentation of an improvised play. Since dialogue is at the heart of every dramatic encounter, whether in theatre or in the classroom, drama in education has enormous potential for the teacher.

Many commentators have emphasised the importance of drama in providing opportunities for language use. Edmiston, Enciso and King, (1987) see drama functioning at the centre of language growth and learning. Patrick Verriour (1985) values dramatic contexts because they give children the means to take control of their own thinking and language. Richard Courtney (1982) demonstrates that dramatic play is a basic activity for the learning of languages at all ages.

All language learning occurs within an interaction of one kind or another. Goleman (1986) points out that our discourse is already social, already in dialogue. Growth lies in becoming a more knowing participant in the social dialogue that constitutes all discourse.

Dialogue in a Drama Context

Recently, I worked with a class of kindergarten and grade one children who had been reading a number of books about school, including *That Dreadful Day* by James Stephenson (1985). This picture book deals with the fears children have about first going to school. I set up the drama in role as principal of the school, and the children became my staff. We had to consider how to induct new children into the life of the school. Together, we considered the problems that might arise, the fears the new children might have, the ways in which we could alleviate anxiety or confusion. The children shared feelings and memories of *their* first days at school, and we talked of ways in which things might have been made easier for them. One boy explained that he was frightened and behaved badly on his first day, because he was afraid that his mother would never return to fetch him.

There were several other adults in the room including the class teacher, an aide and a student teacher. They became the new children. The children, in the roles of teachers, and I observed these new children carefully. We interpreted from their expressions and gestures what they might be feeling and thinking, and what problem, we, as the staff, might face in dealing with them. Then each child was given a group of teachers who would take responsibility for her. The teachers spent a great deal of time and effort explaining school life to the children, introducing them to classroom materials and practices, explaining rules, telling stories, reading to them and helping them to feel comfortable with school. Afterwards, as principal and staff, we reflected on the experience. Some valuable and very practical ideas were offered for dealing with new children, and listed on sheets of paper so that the students' thinking was made visible to them. We also listened to the children as they described what their first day at school had been like.

In this classroom event, some of the key concepts of drama in education were in operation. Children worked in what Dorothy Heathcote (Johnson and O'Neill, 1984) has called 'Mantle of the Expert.' This 'denotes that moment when the teacher deliberately reverses the usual teacher/pupil relationship and bestows expertise on the children' (Havell, 1987: 174). They were in role as responsible adults, with knowledge and ability. I worked as teacher-in-role – the school principal-with the task of supporting, extending, and challenging the children from within the work. Dialogue, both in the imaginary situation, and with reference to the children's real lives, was indeed the cornerstone of the activity. There were real tasks to be done – explaining, persuading, justifying, instructing, reading, sharing stories, showing consideration for others. The dialogue in which we were engaged allowed the students to see themselves as people with competences, as people able to teach as well as to learn; it encouraged them to make explicit their understandings about school, its purposes and their relationship to it.

Theatre Metaphors and Classroom Encounters
When students and teachers are engaged in authentic dialogue, they recreate themselves as listeners and speakers in new classroom script. It is not surprising that the vocabulary of drama and theatre has been borrowed by educators who are committed to dialogue and the kinds of transformations it creates in the social context of the classroom. For example, Nancy R. King (1986) draws a useful analogy between the curriculum as an event and different kinds of theatre experiences. Peter McLaren (1986) calls teaching 'essentially improvised drama' (p114). Madeleine R. Grumet (1978) highlights content when she notes that both teacher and curriculum draw the attention of those in attendance to the forms that are their social, cultural and historical inheritance. Ira Shor (Shor and Freire, 1987) seems to sum up these positions when he says, 'The syllabus is as much a script as it is a curriculum. The classroom is a stage for performance as much as it is a moment of education.' (p116)

Theatre metaphors illuminate an idea of teaching which is essentially dialogue, and therefore dynamic, democratic, social, demystifying and open to change. The puzzling thing is that teachers who are interested in exploring the possibilities of dialogue as a powerful force for teaching and learning so rarely seem to go beyond mere metaphor and use the drama process itself in their classroom. Even teachers with a belief in the importance of story and literature are likely to neglect or overlook the usefulness and significance of dramatic activities.

Drama and theatre are built on a sequence of episodes for opposing voices. We are familiar with Barbara Hardy's (1977) claim that narrative is a primary act of mind. The dramatising power of the human mind is equally basic. The voices in our own mind; our skill in representing the actions and speech of others; our ability to see the other side of things, to create opposing opinions, to be able to anticipate answers to the questions we ask, are all built on our power to dramatise, to put ourselves in someone else's shoes. As Harold Rosen (1980) puts it, 'The imagination can dramatise for our purposes the explorations of our minds' (p162). He has described dramatic behaviour as ordinary, pervasive and universal. For him, it is not an optional extra grafted on to human activity but a common human resource, intrinsic to everyday social behaviour and perhaps even more fundamental than poetry and fiction. 'The dramatic is always lurking below the surface of the flow of inter-action' (p161).

Drama in education offers teachers the opportunity to negotiate the content of the work, alter the relationship between teacher and students, and trans-form the social structure of the classroom.

Curricular Events and Theatrical Events

If we examine the ways in which the vocabulary of theatre has been employed to elucidate the classroom encounter, we may clarify the nature of the drama event, how it can assist in establishing a shared context for learning, and the function of the teacher within the experience.

Nancy R. King (1986) believes that the importance of the social context of the classroom and the personal contexts of individual participants in determin-ing the meaning of classroom events cannot be overemphasised. Like Grumet (1978), she sees the curriculum as an event with many similarities to the theatrical event. Both are staged, bounded in space and time, and take place in special buildings set aside for the purpose. The essence of the class-room event cannot be captured in a lesson plan or a curriculum guide. A drama is not merely the script or the staging and neither is the curriculum a set of strategies or an instructional manual.

Curricular events may be likened to grand opera when they are elaborately staged and based on cultural themes that are well known, recurrent and revered. On some occasions, however, curricular content is improvised in res-ponse to contributions, either welcome or unsolicited, from the learners. At such times, the curriculum resembles another form of dramatic event – street theatre. Curricular events resemble street theatre to the extent that they must be accomplished with sufficient daring and dazzle to hold the attention of people who are on their way elsewhere or who are thinking about other things (p36).

King assumes that the spectator in theatre is necessarily passive. But where the theatre event has grasped the minds and imaginations of the spectator, their passivity will mask an intense inner activity. For Peter Brook (1972), the ideal theatre situation is where the audience feels the same compulsive necessity as the theatre artists. Brook proposes the use of a valuable French word, *assistance*, in outlining the function of the kind of audience he hopes for in the theatre. In French 'I watch a play' translates as 'J'assiste à une pièce.' In English this is the word used to define the function of the congregation at a religious ceremony – the congregation assists at the ritual, it participates, it takes action. In a curricular event in which the students felt the same compulsive necessity as their teachers, the attitudes and activities of everyone in the classroom might be summed up in this notion of assistance.

The purposes and practices of theatre and rituals are closely linked. Peter McLaren (1986) notes that ritual is not mere routine or habit. Rituals, like theatre, do more than display symbolic meanings, but also instrumentally bring states of affairs into being. Ritual and theatre do not merely reflect – they articulate. Although many educators have drawn parallels between schooling and ritual, McLaren points out that the potential of ritual as an explanatory concept in classroom analysis has not been realised. Although ritual relates to classroom instruction, teacher performance, student-teacher interactions, motivation and indoctrination, it may be that as a concept it is still insufficiently defined to be of use to teachers. It lacks the dynamic, dialogic connotations that make theatre metaphors so useful in analysing the classroom encounter.

The Content of the Classroom Dialogue

How will teachers and students create the new script which authentic dialogue requires? Grumet (1978) writes of wrenching 'the forms of the curriculum from their habitations in dead and distant worlds, distilling from the names, the dates, the proofs, the texts what is essential in the particular content to our own experience.' Dialogue has been described by Freire (1972) as 'the sealing together of the teacher and the students in the joint act of knowing and reknowing the object of study' (p100). Dialogic enquiry is situated in the culture, language, politics and themes of the students. However, this kind of enquiry does not merely exploit or endorse the given but seeks to transcend it. Study is situated inside the subjectivity of the students in such a way as to detach students from that very subjectivity into more advanced reflection (Shor and Freire, 1987). Inner reflective activity is fed by dialogue that takes place in context. In my earlier example, the children were released by the dialogue embedded within the drama into new understandings about school and their place in it.

Reflection and distance – both key concepts in education and in theatre – are crucial elements in achieving a sense of judgment and a grasp of alternatives. As Heathcote (in Johnson and O'Neill, 1984) puts it, 'If you cannot increase reflective power in people you might as well not teach, because reflection is the only thing that in the long run changes anybody.' (p104)

Freire (Shor and Freire, 1987) makes clear that a true dialogue is always an enquiry. There is an implied challenge, a refusal to accept the given which makes the process of dialogue and enquiry an emancipatory one. We step back from the situation in order to see it more clearly and to judge it.

The drama process operates in a similar way. It may be that it is really this kind of challenge and the possibility of emancipation implied in the process that prevents some teachers from using drama, rather than the fears about losing control that are so often expressed by teachers. It may be more worrying for the teachers to lose control of the ideas in the classroom than to lose control of children's behaviour. But if teachers want to engage in genuine dialogue with their students they must be prepared for responses which are unpredictable, challenging and transformative. The task for the teacher is to set up concrete situations out of the forms of the curriculum which invite the engaged yet critical actions of the students. Drama, which is built on these kinds of situations, will be the greatest help in achieving this goal. The children involved earlier in teaching were clearly dealing with the forms of the curriculum.

Student Themes and Motivation

An educational dialogue with the power to transform the curriculum into a spontaneous, dynamic event will inevitably be based on themes essential to the students. For Peter McLaren (1988), a pedagogy which elicits dynamic forms of participation will positively resonate with 'the dreams, desires, voices and utopian longings' (p168) of the students. Drama is one of the few areas of the curriculum that is built on these dreams and voices. It works on the premise that the material which students themselves bring to the work is valid. Indeed, drama could not operate without including this kind of material. What would have taken place in the school drama I described earlier if the children had been unable to bring their own ideas to the work? Even when the teacher has launched the work at a point that seems very distant from the student's needs and interests, the spontaneous, negotiated and permeable quality of drama will allow those meanings to emerge.

When I enquired what they would like to do a drama about, a group of eighth grade students in Australia said they didn't care so long as it wasn't about real life. (Apparently they had recently been engaged in a long and intense investigation of the lives of disabled people.) I asked them if Outer Space would be sufficiently far from real life and they agreed that it would.

I began a piece of drama in which the members of the group were astronauts. In role as Head of the Space Centre, I explained that one of our spaceships had not returned from a previous mission to the farthest reaches of the galaxy. We had lost all contact with the ship. Aboard that ship were some of their relatives and friends. I asked the astronauts to volunteer for a rescue mission to the planet where the lost ship had been headed. They agreed to undertake the voyage. When the rescue mission arrived on the planet, I contacted the spaceship in role as an official from the planet, and asked them to take off again immediately. I assured them that their comrades were perfectly happy and did not want to return to earth. The students insisted on meeting the members of the previous expedition, so I asked the two drama teachers present to take on the role of survivors of the first spaceship. The students interrogated them about their new life on the planet, and urged them to return to earth. They assured their rescuers that they were perfectly happy and did not wish to return home. Suddenly, a girl who had been rather uninvolved up to this point in the work stepped forward. 'But father,' she said, speaking directly to one of the teachers, 'I've promised the family that I'll bring you home.' The father shook his head. Immediately the meanings that were being negotiated had a direct connection with the students' real lives, their anxieties, their understandings of loss, their fears and nightmares.

Drama can be a powerful antidote to the kind of alienation many students feel in the school situation, where everything they bring to the educational encounter is ignored or rejected. Authentic dialogue and drama can both be effective weapons against alienation.

Where student interest is seen as valid, the result is a high degree of motivation. According to Ira Shor, the dominant curriculum treats motivation as outside the action of study. 'Tests, discipline, rewards, punishment, the promise of future jobs, are considered the motivating devices, alienated from the act of learning now' (p5). Motivation is seen as a force that can be manipulated externally, rather than as something which grows from the experience of the students, as they live inside and outside the classroom. In Heathcote's view, this kind of curriculum is not authentic. The tasks set are not real. In all her work she has celebrated the power of an apparently unreal activity, drama, to authenticate the curriculum. 'When we reflect on our world ... we are inexorably led eventually to real events, because drama always must deal with the affairs of people' (in Johnson and O'Neill, 1984: 149).

The Teacher as Artist

To overcome the 'destructive arts of passive education' (Shor and Freire, 1987: 116), not only must the script of the traditional classroom be changed, but the function of the teacher must be rearticulated. If we conceive of the curriculum event as resembling theatre, what is the role of the teacher? Is the teacher to be seen as producer, stage manager, director, playwright, designer, performer, or a combination of all of these? Ira Shor suggests that teachers can consider themselves dramatists when they rewrite the routine classroom scripts and reinvent liberating ones. Certainly the drama teacher will function frequently as director. Morgan and Saxton (1987) suggest that when the teacher takes on a role, as I did in both the school and the spaceship dramas, he or she will be working as performer, director and playwright, but from *inside* the work. The notion of teacher as performer is a complex one. Peter McLaren (1986) pointed out the dangers of the teacher operating as performer or, as he defines it, 'teacher-as-entertainer.' But this is emphatically *not* the function of the teacher-in-role. The teacher-as-entertainer may engage the students, but they remain a passive audience of isolated and unreflective spectators. When students remain isolated viewers of the action, they are being entertained.

The entertainer will not be the most effective model for the teacher, but a number of educators have usefully compared the teacher to the artist. Art has been defined as a process in which skills are employed to discover ends through action (Eisner, 1985a). In crafts, on the other hand, skills are employed to arrive at preconceived ends. Shor and Freire (1987) regards the necessary 'problematising' of the material for study, 'the uncovering of key themes and access points to consciousness and then recomposing them into an unsettling critical investigation' (p115) as an artistic process. Freire (*ibid*) agrees that education is simultaneously a political and an aesthetic act. Education is artistic even when it is an act of knowing.

'Teachers who function artistically in the classroom...provide a climate that welcomes exploration and risk-taking.' (Eisner 1985b, 118) The teacher/artist requires flexibility, ingenuity, personal creativity and an ability to exploit opportunities as they occur. To carry out the kind of teaching which is transformative and dialogic, the teacher as artist will also need curiosity, the ability to focus critical reflection, the strength to cope with uneasiness, uncertainty and unpredictability, and considerable tolerance of ambiguity. 'It is in the areas of ambiguity that transformation takes place' (Burke, 1969: xix). In drama, where teachers operate within process as co-artists with the children, they are accustomed to working in this kind of open possibility. In the spaceship drama, I could not have anticipated the personal resonance that the work acquired, but the structure of the work allowed these meanings to emerge.

Like any artist, the drama teacher must be prepared to work with processes that 'proceed in steps and stages, each of them representing an interim result that cannot be connected with the final solution' (Ehrenzweig 1967: 47). Their aesthetic function is heightened when they take on a role in the drama – 'the most subtle strategy available to a teacher' (Bolton, 1984: 135).

Teacher-in-Role and Liminal Servant

The teacher working in role is not acting. This strategy, which has transformed drama teaching in Britain and Canada, has been much discussed and often misunderstood. Rosenberg (1987) mentions it with a total lack of understanding of its educational and dramatic function. 'Assuming a character different from yourself may appeal to you if you have a flair for the dramatic or find it convenient to hide for a time behind another identity' (p37). It is an odd notion that it is appropriate for teachers to indulge their desire to act or wish to hide in another identity, but it is fairly typical of the misunderstandings which Heathcote, in particular, has had to face.

When a teacher works in role it is an act of conscious self-presentation, but one that invites the watchers – the students – to respond actively, to join in, to oppose or transform what is happening. The teacher-in-role unites the students, trades on their feelings of ambivalence and vulnerability and focuses their attention. They have permission to stare, to use Heathcote's phrase. 'As teacher-in-role, her aim was to switch on the watcher in the participant' (Havell, 1987: 173). As Beckerman (1972) puts it, something is happening, something which at first unites the group in contemplation and then engages them in action. As in the theatre, the group in a drama lesson is caught up in a complex pattern of expectation and response. There is the beginning of what has been described as 'an audience mind,' which is affirmed in appropriate response and commitment to what is being presented. The students begin to read the performance of the teacher-in-role, searching for clues about the fictional world which is being born before their eyes, the relationship to the teacher's role, their own role function, and the power they possess within it. 'By taking a role the teacher is in a position to support, challenge and clarify the pupils' responses as the drama progresses' (Havell, 1987: 173). Students are challenged to make sense of what they see, to become aware of their own responses, and to use these responses as an impetus to action. Choice and responsibility grow from action and awareness from the

109

reflection. As in the two drama lessons outlined earlier, dialogue is at the heart of the encounter with the role and response is implicit in the situation.

The Concept of Liminality

The function of this strategy is very close to Peter McLaren's (1986) fascinating and provocative definition of the teacher as liminal servant. Liminality has the connotation of a threshold, a state which is 'betwixt and between.' Liminality, he explains, is a term that refers to a social state in which participants are stripped of their usual status and authority. It is a process of separation and transition. Victor Turner (1969), from whom McLaren borrowed the concept of liminality, writes: 'If liminality is regarded as a time and place of withdrawal from normal modes of social action, it can be seen as potentially a period of objective scrutinisation of the central values and axioms of the culture in which it occurs' (p167).

This is close to Heathcote's description of drama as a no-penalty zone, 'which allows us to stand back and see what it is we are experiencing at any moment ... so that contemplation in flux is possible' (in Johnson and O'Neill, 1984: 192). This notion includes the elements of transition, withdrawal and scrutinisation which are contained in the concept of liminality.

For Heathcote, the factors implied in setting up drama include isolation, particularisation, distortion, and forming, 'Drama must show change... it freezes a problem in time, and you examine the problem as the people go through a process of change' (p115). Drama for Heathcote is essentially a process of transition, of transformation. Withdrawal from the burden of reality allows one freedom to contemplate, to speculate, to construct alternatives. There are changes in time, space and perspective. Liminality, as well as the element of separation, includes that of status reversal. So does drama, as in the example of the children becoming teachers.

Heathcote most often uses teacher-in-role to negotiate an exchange of power with her students. The strategy she calls 'Mantle of the Expert' is also designed to achieve this. It 'denotes that moment when the teacher deliberately reverses the usual teacher/pupil relationship and bestows expertise on the children' (Havell, 1987: 174). Drama provides Heathcote with a fictional context for authentic teaching. 'We have the paradox that art could be a vehicle for changing the work of school to make reality-useable outcomes' (p192).

Characteristics of the Liminal Servant

Much of what McLaren (1988) says about the teacher as liminal servant seems to apply directly to the drama teacher, and particularly to the teacher working in role. I have listed some of the characteristics he regards as necessary for the teacher as liminal servant below on the left. Heathcote's list of tasks for the authentic teacher is on the right:

Characteristics	Tasks
Teaching is a social construction.	Encouraging student interaction and decision-making.
There is an added vitality in the forms of instruction.	Learning to present problems differently to students.
There is a stress on the 'as if' quality of learning.	Establishing a context for learning. Taking more risks with materials.
A felt context is established for the subject matter.	Imagining and carrying out a greater variety of tasks.
Aesthetic truth is prized as much as objective truth.	Giving constant attention to detail.
Liminal servants do not see themselves as instructors or transmitters of knowledge, but allow students to embody or incarnate knowledge.	Engineering a greater variety of reflective techniques. Working with focus and significance to harness students' needs.
They are prepared to become a student of the pupils' needs and desires.	Tolerating ambiguity. Devising fruitful encounters between self, students, ideas, knowledge, and skills.
They teach to discover their own meanings and not merely to share available answers.	Engendering productive tension. Giving power to students.
They cast off authority as speakers so that the students can claim some authority of their own. (p170-175)	Working to bring schools and society together. (p179-186)

McLaren sees the teacher as liminal servant engaging in pedagogical surrealism that attacks the familiar and disturbs commonplace perspectives. This 'defamiliarisation' which McLaren proposes as a function of teaching and learning is identical to Brecht's 'alienation effect' and Shkolovsky's (Lemon and Reis, 1965) view of the techniques of art 'to make objects unfamiliar, to make forms difficult, to increase the difficulty and length of perception because the process of perception is an aesthetic end in itself and must be prolonged.' To disturb commonplace perceptions is central to Heathcote's work.

Her use of 'frame' and 'mantle of the expert' are both strategies to bring about new perspectives. Bolton (1984) describes her work as 'prismatic.' He shows how it challenges the simplicity of context and allows for a state of mind which is both reflective and engaged.

The teacher-in-role would seem to be an exemplar of McLaren's teacher as liminal servant. Working in role, the teacher can lead the group into the imagined world of drama, a place of separation, transition and transformation, where the rules of the classroom are in suspension. In this fictional world, students can alter their status, engage in inquiry and explore alternatives. The teacher-in-role does not merely elicit responses from students, but can challenge, model, support, exploit tensions and shape the experience from within so that it develops transformative power. 'One cannot endow people with commitment to a point of view, but often by placing them in the response position they begin to hold a point of view, because they can see it has power' (Johnson and O'Neill, 1984: 164).

Heathcote has been criticised for using what appears to be a very theatrical and manipulative strategy, but all teachers will have educational intentions, as well as competencies and responsibilities. She writes: 'Teachers do not have a mandate to teach without reflective processes and responsible outcomes' (*ibid*, p198). All education, even liberating education, is directive, as Freire makes clear (Shor and Freire, 1987).

The use of drama and teaching-in-role can transform the classroom into a place where something happens, where there is authentic dialogue between teacher and students. I have tried to show that one of the qualities of drama which allows these changes to take place is its liminality. As Heathcote (in Johnson and O'Neill, 1984) puts it 'the child enters the zone of circumstance permitted by the drama situation, and in shaping the circumstance's future, the child's future is shaped, ready to be available in the real society' (p198).

McLaren (1986) suggests that it is improvident of the curriculum planner not to consider the drama teacher as an invaluable aid in shaping learning potential in the classroom. He goes so far as to suggest that spontaneous drama and creative arts should form the nub of the multidisciplinary curriculum.

Drama in education, structured so that there is an event with content weighted by the needs and interests of the students, and led by a teacher who has the quality of a liminal servant, reaches its ends through dialogue. It is a collective activity, built on imaginative transformation, negotiation, speculation and interpretation. Drama in education is a model for authentic classroom dialogue.

Episode Three
Perspectives on Drama

Episode Three
Perspectives on Drama

After the Inner London Education Authority (ILEA) was disbanded, O'Neill relocated to the US and worked principally with graduate students at the Ohio State University. Here, she was able to flesh out many of the theoretical concerns that had informed her praxis while employed at ILEA as an in-service provider to local drama teachers. During her time in America she completed her doctorate, 'Structure and Spontaneity: Improvisation in Theatre and Education' through the University of Exeter (1991) and was commissioned by the late Lisa Barnett of Heinemann Publishing to develop the 'Dimensions of Series' which addressed issues of theory, practice and research in theatre and drama education. *Drama Worlds: A Framework for Process Drama* (O'Neill, 1995); *Drama for Learning: Dorothy Heathcote's Mantle of the Expert Approach to Education* (Heathcote and Bolton, 1995); *Educational Drama and Language Arts: What Research Shows* (Wagner, 1998) and *Redcoats and Patriots: Reflective Practice in Drama and Social Studies* (Taylor, 1998) are four of the titles in this important series.

O'Neill was in a strong position to influence American drama education. She was a popular charismatic speaker across the US and beyond, and sat on numerous curriculum and examination committees where she advocated for drama in education. Exceedingly generous, she would often invite those students needing financial support to stay in her apartment in Columbus, Ohio, permitting them to enrol in her influential summer schools for little or no charge.

The summer schools were especially unique in that they provided extended periods of time for educators to experience and deconstruct process drama. During one summer (1989) O'Neill's students consisted of teachers from Australia, Canada, England, Ireland and the US. She began the week-long drama in a similar vein to *The Recruiting Officer* (see Introduction), inviting the

114

participants to share some of the themes they would like to explore and to discuss their expectations.

The group agreed that they would be itinerants, dreamers, in search of a better world. In role as a shadowy leader of the drama which became known as *The Quest*, O'Neill claimed that she could only take them on half of the journey and that they would meet someone who would be responsible for taking over from her. The implications of this news did not register with the nomads as they informed loved ones of their plans and began their eager preparations for embarkation. As perilous as the adventure initially seemed, including delicate negotiation of various agendas, grappling with hazardous terrain and fending off imminent threats, the group bonded as a community in the hope that ultimately they would find the bliss they were searching for.

When the leader suddenly disappeared with no one to take over, uncertainty came to the surface and anxiety increased. The stakes were raised considerably when deciding to continue; the dreamers entered a land where they had to renounce a favourite memory. For some, this challenge was too much; they were ill-prepared for it and decided to return home. Others reluctantly gave up their memories whether these were of home, friendships or family, and ventured forth.

Finally, after wending their way through a treacherous ravine, they came across a wizened mystical figure, sitting isolated on the top of a hill, who seemed to hold the truth of what the remaining wanderers were seeking. 'Ah, so you have arrived at the end of your arduous travel,' said O'Neill in role, and delivered weakly with some pain. 'I cannot promise you what you will find behind me, it may be what you are in search of, and it may not. For I have travelled long and hard like you, but, alas, cannot take the final step. For it is clear that those who go forth shall never return. No one comes back.' The dreamers had made many friendships during their quest but now decisions had to be made. It was an agonising moment as some decided to go forward while others, uncertain for the first time, sat with the crusty old figure at the top of the mountain, doomed to spend the rest of their days questioning the choice they had made and wondering whether inner contentment really did exist beyond.

A unique aspect of this structure was the improvised manner in which the process drama unfolded. Improvisation is occurring throughout: from the initial meeting with the shady leader to the conversations with loved ones, the re-enactments of the painstaking journey, and the final encounter with the owlish harridan. Participants are assuming roles and attitudes, working without a script and generating their own relationship to the material. The teacher of the process drama commits to the possibilities which emerge from spontaneous encounters. The landscape of *The Quest* process drama is driven by an ability to release the imagination, to accept the constraints in which the art has been structured and to make discoveries that could not be predicted but rather emerge in process. In this respect, improvisation in process drama permits participants to develop sustained and prolonged experiences with the thematic material, and then implicates participants in the theatrical world. If the participants are constructing the content and form, in partnership with their teacher, then inevitably all are going to have greater control over the script which is generated in action. One way of achieving ownership and belief in drama is through improvisation.

O'Neill has written widely about how extemporaneous actions and gesture need to be layered into process drama. She has examined the theories of Artaud, Brook, Littlewood, Johnstone and Stanislavski, among others, and how their notions of improvised activity and an organic episodic structure can yield fertile discoveries.

> Improvised activities have the potential to develop a life of their own when they develop beyond the level of exercise, game, or training and when dramatic worlds are encouraged to grow in accordance with the rules of the medium. When the work transcends didactic or technical purposes and achieves a satisfying sense of form and coherence, while retaining the genuine immediacy, spontaneity, ingenuity, and playfulness that are among its essential characteristics, it will indeed be a genuine process (O'Neill, 1995: 12)

Although the teacher is playing along as a co-artist, assessing the form's merits and searching for devices that will strengthen the encounter, she is also encouraging the participants to be accountable for their own actions. It is not that anything goes in the name of spontaneity, but how one's responses logically help build dramatic context. O'Neill is keen that participants recognise how to make good offers, not to reject or block, but activate their imaginations while at the same being open to surprise and discovery. For instance, when the leader suddenly disappears in *The Quest*, when cherished memories are to be surrendered and as the dreamers are ultimately confronted with a disturbing dilemma – either sit with the crusty old fool at the top of the mountain for the rest of your life or go forward and never return – participants are entrapped in the web of form that they both submit to and control. They began their adventure eagerly, but now they have got what they least bargained for and have to live with their decisions.

116

It is important to note how O'Neill is building dramatic tension into the process drama through the teacher-in-role strategy. She argues that this is quite different from introducing conflict which can lead to fairly stereotypical and artificial responses. She elevates the teachers' artistry as they work toward cognitive and emotional engagement, and as they search for the tasks that maintain genuine involvement. 'Encounters with the teacher-in-role,' she writes, 'are likely to generate tension, particularly if the role appears ambiguous, obstructive or untrustworthy' (1997: 97). O'Neill knows how dramatic irony operates in the theatre as a structural device to draw the audience in and, equally, draw them out. 'For students, interpreting the possible intentions of such a role and responding appropriately is a source of immediate tension within the group. Should this person be trusted? What is their real purpose?' What the participants may least expect can harness their attention. When they are thrown into states of disequilibria, when unforeseen challenges surprisingly occur, they are forced to draw upon their own inner resources, to get themselves out of the mess.

The chapters which follow expand upon O'Neill's interest in assisting teachers to build a dramatic vocabulary which enables them to understand their craft more coherently. Drama, she reminds us, is about making futures, and heightening teachers' capacity to develop multiple, shifting and evolving perspectives on the material. Theatre teachers for the future require the ability to thoroughly research their discipline and to generate their own theoretical frameworks. Always conscious of the pioneers in the field, O'Neill advocates for grounding in the related disciplines of philosophy, psychology, anthropology and sociology; nonetheless, it will be in the theatre and performance studies where educators will be mostly informed and enriched.

Sometimes the best kind of encounters occur when teachers feel comfortable slowing the drama down, activating the students' critical eye to explore what is happening in the immediate present. Never one to want to hurry along to the next activity, O'Neill is quite comfortable developing the perceptual ability of the group to carefully notice the thematic import of the material and how the adept manipulation of dramatic form can yield resonate images. She is not interested in simplistic readings of complex events; what important is that the group tolerate diverse perspectives. Sometimes it is better to be left with nagging questions and uncertain futures than to have pat answers and unrealistic solutions. If the group is going to be empowered in the process, if their own readings of the material are to be privileged and if they are going to be released out of passive states and become active and reflective artists, then leaders have to structure for spontaneity. But such structuring will always be informed by the teachers' theoretical perspective, and by the aesthetic and pedagogical principles which they believe are truly transformative.

> From the moment of its inception, the spontaneity of process drama is supported, contained, and articulated by the embryo at its core – its inherent dramatic structure. When process drama develops in harmony with the principles of theatre form, when an understanding of dramatic structure gives unity and coherence to the work, and when the spontaneous experience is not subverted by pressures of audience, end-product, or limited instrumental demands, it becomes possible for it to evolve into a significant dramatic event, as immediate, engaging, and necessary as the best of any other kind of theatre. (O'Neill, 1995: 13)

8

Artists and Models

Originally published as 'Artists and Models: Theatre Teachers for the Future' in *Design for the Arts in Education*, March/April 1991: 23-27.

As theatre implies an audience, so teaching implies learning. Both activities are essentially dialogues. 'The work of art is a challenge to the performance of a like act of evocation and organisation, through imagination, on the part of the one who experiences it' (Dewey, 1934: 274).

If something is to be taught successfully, the subject matter should evoke a response in the learner that is accepted and understood. To teach is to bring the learner into active participation in the event. As Edmund Feldman (1970) wrote, 'learning is contingent upon a dialogue in which we feel ourselves addressed and answered, especially in the arts'(p145).

It is not surprising that the vocabulary of theatre has been borrowed by educators who are committed to dialogue and to the kinds of transformations it creates in the social context of the classroom. Theatre metaphors illuminate an idea of teaching that is essentially dialogic and therefore dynamic, democratic, social, demystifying and open to transformation. Ideally, one might expect that theatre teaching would itself exemplify this kind of dialogic approach. If dialogue is an exchange of views, then we may have to acknowledge that much teaching in both schools and universities, even in theatre departments, is delivered in the form of a monologue. This model of teaching is perhaps less frequently used at the graduate level but, during their training, teachers are likely to have to listen to many monologues on subject-based and professional topics and, in turn, to develop information packages or monologues for their own future use. The shortcomings of the popular notion of teaching as the delivery of pre-packaged units to the students are revealed

119

by overemphasis on the activity of the teacher and underemphasis on the activity of the learner. Passivity on the part of the student is inimical to any kind of effective teaching and, in particular, makes nonsense of attempts to teach the arts.

As Lloyd Ultan (1989) wrote, 'Arts education addresses the development of human skills, perceptions, and attitudes that, in the long term, can revolutionise human experience' (p73). Arts educators have at their disposal a range of ideas, materials and approaches for the exploration, articulation and representation of experience. If arts education, at whatever level, is carried on by the kind of transmission models that prevail in our schools and universities, then the case for including the arts in the curriculum will be seriously weakened.

Theatre Teachers for the Future

Theatre departments that undertake teacher education are faced by a number of challenges. It will not be easy to find the right balance of creation, performance, criticism, and scholarship for an effective dramatic curriculum for K-12 theatre teachers, but this task is essential if theatre education itself is to survive into the next century.

Difficult as it is to decide what we want future theatre teachers to know, it is even more difficult to define what kind of teachers we want them to be. We must attempt to produce theatre teachers who are not merely knowledgeable and skilful in teaching young people about theatre, but who can motivate, activate, and empower students in and through theatre. We need theatre teachers who, rather than relying on performance skills, are animators able to activate and engage students in learning experiences. Theatre and learning both require conditions to be deliberately set up in which significant experiences can occur. A genuine encounter with theatre and an experience of learning can be a process of discovery and a process that can provide both a powerful sense of disclosure and illumination and a feeling of growing insight and mastery.

Theatre teachers whose aim is to set up shared learning experiences with their students start with an advantage. The medium in which they operate is necessarily dialogic and demands active human presence and participation. While encouraging identification, it promotes distance and reflection – key concepts in the arts and in learning. But this advantage brings with it responsibilities that must be honoured.

The arts represent a different way of knowing and responding to the world. Among the qualities that make them special is their ability to give a voice to students, to allow students to locate their own experience in relationship to the art form and its heritage, and to give validity to the kinds of knowledge and experience the students bring with them to the classroom. These qualities alone will make it vital to retain vigorous, creative and effective arts teaching in our schools.

Teacher Models

Teachers are both communicators and models. Perhaps the biggest influence on teachers is the memory of their own schooling. The next most important influence is likely to be the kind of teacher encountered in their own training. This carries implications for any future recruits to the professorship in theatre education. During their training, theatre students are likely to have encountered instructors who as models may represent a less than ideal paradigm. In dance, for example, much training centres on corrections, and dancers who do not receive this kind of attention from their teachers may feel neglected and overlooked. This kind of practice will be familiar to some acting students. But however useful one might claim this approach to be in technical training, it is a deficit model with an emphasis on correcting errors rather than helping students to discover what they can do.

When teaching art, the teacher necessarily demonstrates the personal and professional qualities that are being encouraged. The willingness to be involved, to engage in dialogue, to take risks as well as to encourage risk-taking in students, to venture into the unknown, to court mystery, to tolerate anxiety and ambiguity – these are the qualities that should pervade the theatre teacher's approach to students.

The student invariably learns about the teacher as well as from the teacher. Effective teachers in any subject area will be human events, not transmission devices and will model and embody the very attitudes and values being fostered.

Teacher and Artist

The teaching of any arts subject and, in particular, the group processes that lead to theatre, is a cognitively sophisticated and demanding activity. It involves a subtle attention to detail, nuance and implication; the ability to exploit the unpredictable in the course of the work; the confidence to shift both educational and artistic goals where appropriate; and the security to deal with disappointment and possible failure. A key factor is the ability to set up the kind of conditions in which students can encounter the art form directly and through which they can experience the exhilaration of the search for and discovery of new ideas, capacities, forms and interpretations. In theatre, the crucial ability to work through others and the skill to make positive use of the creative impulses of everyone in the group are essential requirements.

In order to work effectively with students in theatre at any level, the teacher must operate inside the process. For the artist, this stance is inevitable. For the teacher of the arts, it has not always been seen as a necessity. But if we operate as artists for even part of our professional life, it seems prodigal not to use our creative capacities in our teaching. Is it not possible to bring the same kind of aesthetic approach and sensibility to our dialogue with students? If we do attempt to function as artists with our students, a realignment of our working relationships will be essential. As Viola Spolin, (1963: 8) notes, one is seeking a relationship in which

> ... attitudes permit equality between student and teacher and the dependencies of teacher for student and student for teacher are done away with. The problems within the subject matter will teach both of them.

It is unlikely that theatre teachers will be able to operate in these complex processes if their own training in the arts has been safe, stale, repetitive, commercially minded and product-oriented, and where the only challenges to be faced are those of competition, evaluation, and a marketable end product.

Course Content

Any teaching of art must draw its essential content from the very nature of art itself. Clearly, prospective theatre teachers will need a thorough understanding of the nature of theatre. It will not be enough to ensure that they encounter the practical aspects of theatre. Merely engaging in practical tasks does not necessarily lead to understandings and insights. We should not confuse practical activity with learning.

It will be important to remember that we are working with students so that they themselves will become successful teachers. This may require a further rethinking of our practice. At present, a large part of practical theatre training is likely to consist of the experience of being part of a group that has some particular theatre task to perform. Students may learn to operate effectively as members of a creative group, but this experience by itself will not help them to become structure operators who can set up meaningful learning experiences for others.

Dorothy Heathcote (Johnson and O'Neill, 1984), that remarkable teacher of educational drama, proposed that teachers should aim to understand the true rules of the medium of theatre. These she defines as not merely the 'narrow' ones of stage effects, but the study of how meanings are revealed and made explicit in drama and theatre. For Lin Wright (1985), the focus of the dramatic curriculum for teachers should be on the ability to understand and create dramatic form.

It should be possible to set up a dramatic curriculum for prospective teachers that explores the making of meaning in theatre by a true balance between creation, performance, appraisal and contextual knowledge and that presents these aspects in an active and dialogic way. It will be important to recognise, above all, that K-12 theatre teachers need to be able to motivate and engage students of different ages in an active relationship with theatre practices, forms and knowledge. This means that the focus of their own training must be on the processes by which theatre comes into being and on the ways in which a context of true dialogue can be created in the classroom.

Improvisation
A powerful instrument at hand is, I suspect, underused in the training of theatre teachers, although it has proved its use in industrial, managerial, military and therapeutic settings. This instrument is improvisation.

Improvisation provides the possibility of an immediate and prolonged experimental engagement with the dramatic medium. At its most articulate, this spontaneous encounter develops an inner logic and necessity that resembles the logic and necessity of theatre and proceeds without the constraints of a script, an end product or a formal audience. If the teacher works with an understanding of dramatic tension and structure, it will be possible to achieve in improvisation the same dynamic organisation that gives form to theatre experience. Efforts to give shape to the creative experience will be supported by this understanding and by exploiting the kinds of structural devices that playwrights have used. The product or dramatic effect in improvisation, as in more conventional kinds of theatre, comes into being from a prolonged series of transactions among its co-creators and co-recipients.

The creative and essentially dialogic processes of improvisation can provide a generic model for both teaching and learning. The teacher who has an understanding of the true uses of improvisation can harness students' imaginations, create dramatic contexts for learning in other subject areas, provide complex language opportunities and give significant dramatic experience.

The Context of the Theatre Department

A theatre department might need to confront the following questions:

- How can teacher education be fully integrated into the work of the department?

- What new courses are needed and how can these be structured to give prospective teachers the knowledge, skills and artistry to shape dialogic experiences for their own future students?

- What kinds of product and what ways of showing and sharing are valued in the department?

- What kinds of mutually enriching relationships can be set up with local school systems?

- Have successful theatre teachers been identified in the local community and are the skills and insights of these teachers available to the theatre department?

- Are local schools used, not merely as locations for field experience, but as settings for active and cooperative research and development?

- Does research that is recognised and valued in the department venture into problematic areas of classroom research?

- Have relevant and exciting colleagues and courses in other departments been identified; for example, those in anthropology, social studies, literature, communications, psychology and child development?

- Have genuinely dialogic relationships been created between the theatre faculty and these other departments and, in particular, between the theatre and education departments?

Conclusion

Teachers who return for graduate qualification and certification in theatre may not have ambitions in scholarship, but they will have needs related to their knowledge of the subject and their ability to motivate and engage their students in learning. The theatre department will have to provide both for their professional needs as teachers and for their continuing needs as learners. Somehow, their personal and professional development must be integrated. We need to promote and keep alive the active, playful, problem-solving and dialogic qualities of the arts in our teachers and students. This implies that persons engaged to work in the department should be able to model and evoke those qualities. Our lessons about teaching should be implicit in our own teaching methods. We should not teach the teachers one way and expect them to teach another. The content and method of our courses should be relevant directly or indirectly to the practical business of teaching theatre successfully in schools at every level.

Theatre education at its best can provide competencies, insights and a set of processes that will help young people to face the challenges and opportunities that lie ahead. If we neglect to strengthen their imaginations, develop their moral and social perspectives, build their cooperative skills and empower them to construct alternative ways of knowing and participating in the world, our students will be impoverished and disadvantaged in ways that neither money nor privilege nor any social or political remedies can alleviate. Susanne Langer (1953: 306) described drama as the 'mode of destiny.' We can use both drama and theatre to help our students realise their potential, fulfil their destiny and become makers of the future.

9

Theory and Research in Drama

Originally published as 'Into the Labyrinth: Theory and Research in Drama' in Taylor, P. (ed) (1996) *Researching Drama and Arts Education: Paradigms and Possibilities*. London: Falmer Press.

We have been working for several decades in drama in education to establish a sound theoretical base and a productive conceptual framework for our research and practice. In every discipline, the development of theory is critical for both understanding and practical dissemination. Research is generated, guided and enlarged by theory, the lens that focuses and illuminates our complex and multi-layered practice.

Theory provides the instruments through which we discover underlying similarities, patterns and relationships in our work, and articulate these patterns for others. It furnishes lucid images of the characteristics and processes of drama and is fundamental in guiding and shaping our research as it is organised and displayed through the numerous alternative research paradigms now available.

The Relationship of Theory to Practice

It is certainly possible to engage in effective practice without a basis in theory and to undertake theoretical studies without any understanding of practice. We are probably all familiar with examples of this imbalance, perhaps even in our own work. Theatrical performance proliferated in the Middle Ages but, until the rediscovery of Aristotle, there was no theoretical net to throw over it. The absence of theory did not reduce the number or effectiveness of the plays of that period. In *The Quest of Avenues*, Borges describes an Arab philosopher who is familiar with Aristotle's *Poetics* but lacks any conception of the meaning of 'tragedy' and 'comedy' because of the Muslim taboo on representation.

Even when he encounters theatre, he cannot grasp its meaning or its relationship to his knowledge of Aristotle's text. He possesses the net, but can catch nothing in it (Eco, 1994: 102).

I worked in drama for a long time before I began to weave a net of theory to throw over my work, or even to recognise the value of doing so. The significance of theory to the growth and clarification of my own practice became apparent when I encountered Gavin Bolton's work and watched him prepare the ground for so much subsequent theorising in the field. As he began to classify the modes of dramatic activity in the classroom, my own practice began to come into focus (Bolton, 1979). I continue to weave my net, inevitably full of holes, from the ideas of everyone whose work I have encountered in practice or on the page. Woven into this net are all the insights and responses of the teachers and students who have guided or followed me into a myriad of drama worlds.

The most exciting moments occur when theoretical insight clarifies a knotty problem in practice, or when the obscurity of theory is illuminated by a significant memory from the classroom or stage. The loneliest times are when practice inexplicably breaks down, and when the words of thinkers who have spoken clearly to others remain opaque. Still one struggles, accumulating notes, piling up academic papers and suffering, as Theodore Roethke (1977) puts it in his poem *Dolor*, the 'inexorable sadness of pencils' and all the 'misery of manila folders' (p376). It is easy to lose one's sense of direction and purpose in the struggle.

Finding Problems and Questions

The most daunting task for any researcher, however experienced, is to settle on the question, problem or hypothesis that will generate the most fruitful research and bring about the greatest enlargement of the field. These questions and problems are embedded in the context of previous theory and investigation. In my own case, they occur as a result of reflections on what I have read, particularly in dramatic theory, criticism and aesthetics; on the work of others that I have observed and analysed; on emerging patterns in my own work and on the relationships between all of these. Sometimes a word or phrase in the works of some commanding intellect will seize my attention and direct my thought. For example, Langer's assertion that drama is the 'mode of destiny' was the beginning of a fascination with the operation of dramatic time in both process drama and theatre (Langer, 1953). Robert Witkin's understanding that a teacher of the arts need not operate outside the creative event drew me to reflect on the functions of the teacher-in-role

(Witkin, 1974). Hornby's insights about role-playing within the role confirmed my certainty that drama not only happens through role-play but is essential play (Hornby, 1986).

Whatever the focus of our research, we are never working in a vacuum, and our efforts must rest firmly on those of our predecessors if we are not to find ourselves ceaselessly reinventing the wheel. Knowledge and understanding in either science or art do not appear in a vacuum. They spring from an immersion in existing practice and theory, and an appreciation of the central traditions, rules, demands and possibilities in the field. Problem finding is as important as problem solving. We seek, formulate and explicate significant questions that are at the heart of our subject but have not yet made an impact on practice.

Surveying the Field

The first task for every researcher or theorist is to survey the field as thoroughly as possible. This is a daunting task in drama, where concerns connect with so many other domains. An inductive survey may require us to develop at least a passing familiarity with the language of several other disciplines. Philosophy, psychology, anthropology and sociology have all been usefully pressed into service to illuminate our practice in drama and to guide us towards appropriate research paradigms. Although these and other disciplines have served us well, we have not always recognised that the most useful sources of illumination and enrichment may lie closest at hand – for example, in theatre and performance studies.

When we attempt to draw on disciplines remote from our own in their focus, origin, period and discourse, we may betray our lack of understanding and bring confusion to ourselves and our readers. These forays may actually lead us away from the heart of our own work. The more unfamiliar the ground on which we try to build our theories, the more unstable and ephemeral the results are likely to be. This may be the price we pay for importing into our work ideas from distant disciplines and exotic fields of thought. Rigorous reflection is needed to ensure that we are not misunderstanding or misrepresenting the original significance of these studies and distorting them to suit our purposes.

Where a thorough grasp of other disciplines is achieved, fresh understandings and perspectives will clarify, articulate and enlarge our thinking about drama. We will attain an intellectually precise method of writing and talking about our work without having to resort to the creation of restrictive and separatist jargon, or to hijacking inappropriate modes of discourse from more fashionable or 'respectable' disciplines.

As theoretical principles and research frameworks gradually begin to arise from the growth of knowledge and experience in the field, the next effort is to maintain as clear and precise a focus as possible. It is important to remember that research and scholarship cannot be about *everything*. Great intellectual enterprises will fail unless they are accompanied by a sense of perspective and a capacity for prioritising, selecting and organising one's efforts. One must also try to maintain one's interest in and delight in the work so that, in George Eliot's words, our consciousness may be 'rapturously transformed into the vividness of a thought'. Otherwise our undertakings may come to resemble the sterile labours of Eliot's Mr Casaubon in *Middlemarch*, the prototype of the dry, life-denying academic, uselessly accumulating detail for his unwritten masterpiece, *The Key to all Mythologies*, and losing both his direction and his joy in the work. Aesthetic endeavour may be as demanding and, at times, as apparently barren and futile as this arid scholarship but its aim, at least, is generative. Yeats (1923) writes of the work of the artist, but it might also be of the scholar, in this striking image:

> How many centuries spent the sedentary soul
> In toils of measurement, beyond eagle or mole,
> Beyond hearing or seeing or Archimedes' guess
> To raise into being this loveliness? (p357)

Time, observation, intuition, measurement and the guess are all part of the labour of the sedentary soul, as are the multiple perspectives gained by soaring like the eagle and digging like the mole. Every scholar, researcher or artist must maintain a sense of perspective. A keen survey of the landscape is essential before one aspect or feature of the vista captures the gaze. To develop the metaphor, at first the flora may seem to yield most interest but, in the process of surveying the field, the fauna may force itself more strongly on one's attention. In other words, with a deeper knowledge of the domain, the research topic is almost bound to alter. It is futile and unscholarly to attempt to determine a question or problem before knowing the field. Matthew Arnold's precept was to let the mind play freely around the subject until a focus emerged.

The selection of research problems and topics and the questions we raise will inevitably expose our training and our influences and reveal our deepest personal and cultural beliefs and values. Choice always has a moral aesthetic as well as a cognitive dimension. Theory and research can never be neutral.

All knowledge is a social construction, contextual, transient and open to re-construction. Our theory and practice will inevitably reflect contemporary taste, practice and discourse, with all their associated limitations and pre-judices. The shreds and patches of these influences, ideas and values are gradually woven into our individual theoretical net. If they wished to make the effort, it would not be difficult for readers to identify my influences, values, intellectual training and habits of mind from this chapter alone.

The Scientific and the Aesthetic

Values are not necessarily disconnected from and opposed to facts and knowledge. Although a destructive separation of the rational and the affective has persisted for centuries, values and commitments are no longer regarded as essentially irrational and anti-cognitive. This is good news for us in drama since we are concerned with a medium that cannot depend for its life on facts alone. In the light of changing patterns of research in education and the humanities, we need no longer apologise for drama's subjective character, the complexity of the activity and the multi-layered experience to which it gives rise.

Like scientific research, our research in drama demands careful observation, generalisation and the expression of results in a community of scholars and educators. Like science, the study of drama requires detail and precision and will emphasise certain fundamental processes. Thinking creatively and critically, solving problems, constructing knowledge, reading results and developing productive theories are as essential for development in the arts as in the sciences.

The myth persists in some quarters that scientific research is value-free, although Polanyi (1962) has effectively demonstrated that scientific thinking is as personal as it is objective. Scientific knowledge, like knowledge about drama, is symbolic in nature, socially negotiated and, to a significant degree, dependent on imagination and intuition – Archimedes' guess. Scientists need to have some imaginative sense of their theories as a whole before they can set about proving their truth, and the most prized quality for those working in the most rigorous reaches of pure mathematics and theoretical physics is intuition, the feeling for the answer in advance of the proof.

Scientific thinking has a strongly heuristic side and the process of theorising can be both creative and aesthetic. The scientific method itself, like any other explanatory process, is a dialogue between fact and fancy, the actual and the possible, between what could be true and what is in fact the case. It is the

131

story of justifiable beliefs about possible worlds (Medawar, 1982, 111). There is no reason why the mental processes involved in the study of drama should be any less coherent and progressive than those required by the study of science. A precisely similar training of the mind should take place and a similar sense of the essential coherence and parameters of the subject should emerge. The enterprise of drama, as of the other arts, involves, in Shelley's phrase, 'imagining what we know' and recasting our perceptions of the world into aesthetic experience.

Rich and exact description, logical argument and clarity of thought are significant in the pursuit of every kind of research. Questioning, decoding, deducing, comparing, synthesising, interpreting and reasoning are all involved. Theory is never merely a matter of cataloguing processes, patterns and relationships, nor is it generated solely out of observation and experience. Theorists have the freedom to reflect, speculate, imagine, simplify, categorise, infer, exemplify and invent, and the result of their efforts is likely to be successful insofar as these freedoms are entertained. Many influential thinkers, from Nietzsche to Barthes, have been distinguished by their playfulness and irony and, in our efforts to gain respect in the wider academic community, we should not allow ourselves to lose this aspect of our work and become trapped in the toils of measurement. We should not assume that scientific inquiry is the only legitimate form for our research, and neglect or abandon those qualities that I believe are inherent in our subject.

Research Characteristics

The most effective research in drama will share a number of the characteristics of scientific research. General principles are generated and refined by focusing on the central concerns of our subject. Effective and fruitful research will develop emerging representations of the ways in which drama operates in a variety of contexts. These principles and the research to which they give rise are not final truths but approximations. Theorists in science also construct generalisations and approximations. Niels Bohr (Pippard, 1986) reminds us that the task of physics is not to find out how nature is. Instead, 'Physics concerns what we can say about nature' (p46). The scientific community develops constructs, and these are formulated and imposed on natural phenomena in an effort to interpret and explain them. The rapid changes in scientific thinking demonstrate that these constructs are not final truths about the physical world and its attributes. In drama we are dealing with imagined worlds, and the constructs we impose upon these worlds will always remain approximate.

Some subjects, for example the study of history, can be both a science and an art. Scientific principles are involved in the historian's treatment of evidence, and the presence of these elements is what helps to distinguish history from myth, legend and propaganda. Scientific implies systematic, logical and progressive. A scientific approach to any subject changes its character from the casual to the causal, from the random to the systematic. But this kind of approach also implies a sense of consolidating progress. Theory and research may begin in the background of the work and, as they proceed, start organising the foreground as well. There is nothing in these notions of logic and progression that makes them inherently antagonistic to enquiry in drama. Sterile and inappropriate number-crunching is not necessarily implied.

If scientific concepts have significance for an art process, aesthetic concerns may also have relevance for science. Many scientists take a strongly aesthetic view of their enterprises. They point out that there are awkward problems, ugly theories and messy results, and see a definite correlation between the ugly and the wrong. Philip Anderson (1994), the Nobel prize-winning physicist, believes the aesthetic principle operates powerfully in science. The breadth and significance of the work, the subtle and unexpected connections it makes to other fields and the depth to which it delves into nature are among the essentially aesthetic considerations Anderson uses to establish the significance of enquiry. He sees the idea of broken symmetry in physics as having much in common with the literary meaning of the term ambiguity, that is, the number of layers of meaning that can be crammed into one idea. It is not easy to associate ambiguity with what we may be accustomed to admiring as the clarity and logic of the scientific approach.

Questions and Hypotheses

Finding the central questions that will guide their studies is the toughest part of the endeavour for most researchers. Drama offers almost too rich an array of topics and potential lines of inquiry. What's happening in drama? How does it happen? Where does it come from? Who is in charge? What ideas are in play? What kinds of communication arise? Who talks? How much? What about? Who listens? How does drama relate to other kinds of performance? To educational theories? To narrative? To text? To other art forms? Even these few apparently basic and simple questions may be far too wide for a single study and will inevitably generate many further questions. The guiding problem or question must be refined and clarified before it can be serviceable in research.

We must guard against the temptation to consider only problems to which we already know the answers. These questions are inauthentic. Although they may confirm our beliefs, no surprises will occur along the way and no real discoveries will be made. It may be more genuinely authentic and aesthetic, if rather terrifying, to pose a problem for which there may be no final answers. It will be a true quest, although it may not endear us to our supervisors or colleagues.

Having developed a hypothesis, which is after all only an instrument, a guide, we must also guard against allowing ourselves to become possessed by it. As Sterne (1983) reminds us in his ironical masterpiece, *Tristram Shandy*,

> It is in the nature of a hypothesis... that it assimilates everything to itself as proper nourishment; and, from the first moment of your begetting it, it generally grows the stronger by everything you see, read, or understand. That is of great use. (p110)

Once we have developed a hypothesis, a set of criteria, a model or a pattern, the temptation is to locate at all costs more and more instances that seem to fit our pattern. Every occasion or event is seized upon as yet another example of the truth of our theory or model or hypothesis. We crush them into our hypothesis or model like the ugly sisters' toes into the glass slipper. We distort examples that do not quite fit the model or overlook those that form a different pattern entirely. When we find ourselves declaring that apples are in fact oranges, or dismissing them as faulty oranges, we know we are in danger. The trick is to develop as great a scepticism about our own hypothesis as about those of others, and remain flexible in testing alternatives. When these mental habits are not cultivated, even sensitive and knowledgeable researchers descend into fiction, advocacy, gainsaying and delusion.

The Labyrinth
The research question or topic crouches like the Minotaur at the centre of the labyrinth of scholarship, with a maze of pathways and blind alleys leading off in all directions. The words of the great scholars who have gone before us echo distractingly in the gloom. Where is the Ariadne's thread that will guide us? It is unlikely that we will be able to approach our goal by a direct route. Instead, it may be best to seek it indirectly, uncovering assumptions, raising questions, looking up quotations, following footnotes and pursuing intuitions. The metaphor of the researcher as hero struggling to find a way through the labyrinth seems an illuminating one.

This chapter has already employed at least two other metaphors, the net of theory and the field of study. Metaphor is a device for seeing something in terms of something else. It can supply us with a range of new perspectives on our topic. The nature of even the simplest object will be clarified by considering it from as many viewpoints as possible. Metaphor suggests diverse modes and approaches to enquiry. It calls imagination into play, the cognitive capacity that allows us to construct alternative worlds. It is the very enterprise of drama.

Increasingly, researchers are being encouraged to turn to metaphor and imagination in order to resolve or bypass long-standing conflicts between the quantitative and the qualitative, the subjective and the objective. These approaches reconcile old oppositions by linking theory and experience together in new and dynamic ways, helping us to attend to a multiplicity of voices and to interpret what we encounter from a plurality of points of view. Open structures of thought and practice that are always in the process of reconstruction and never promise final resolution are advocated. As Merleau-Ponty (1967) puts it, rationality implies that 'Perspectives blend, perceptions confirm each other, a meaning emerges' (pxix-xx). When various experiences intersect, we weave our past experiences into those of the present and other people's lives into our own.

It is frustrating that so many researchers, including those on university PhD committees, still seem to believe that quantitative methods carry more weight, more truth, and are more persuasive than other methods. In *The Journal of Creative Behaviour*, for instance, surely an obvious arena for potentially creative and adventurous research paradigms, the quantitative seems by far the most acceptable method of enquiry. What is this urge to pin down creativity with numbers? Is there a strict ratio between the elusiveness of a subject and the stringency (and inappropriateness) of the kinds of measurements applied to it?

The Laboratory of Drama

We should be encouraged in our pursuit of the aesthetic and metaphoric, not just by the scientists and researchers who operate in this way but by the fact that many theorists in a variety of subject areas use drama as a model or metaphor for their own thinking. Burke, Goffman and Burns, among others, have viewed their subject through the lens of drama. Drama provides a tight structure or paradigm for human behaviour, an experimentally controlled example of human interaction. Our research site, the field of drama, is itself a laboratory. People are segregated in a space, sometimes the theatre, sometimes a studio or classroom, where human behaviour can be displayed and manipulated through metaphor, repetition and exaggeration. Drama is not a model of every kind of human action but always of the most perplexing, problematic and forbidden activities. It is not surprising if our research is also perplexing and problematic.

We can use graphic means, perhaps even another model, to explicate the drama model. The advantage of constructing models and diagrams is that they are simple, graphic representations of the structure of an idea or process. A model provides the outline of an action or event and has the advantage of brevity and precision. It should be as broadly applicable as possible if it is to be useful in focusing subsequent attempts at investigation, criticism or interpretation.

I find it difficult to think graphically. Charts, graphs, columns and models are almost always lost on me. Their necessary simplicity seems to call too much into question and yet, the more complex they are, the more they may distort what they are supposed to clarify. However, occasionally I see a graphic representation that assists in organising my perceptions. A recent example is the figure in States' (1994) book, *The Pleasure of the Play*, reprinted below. These simple, overlapping circles resonate for me with the separate yet linked episodes of process drama, and it might be possible to adapt the figure to that purpose.

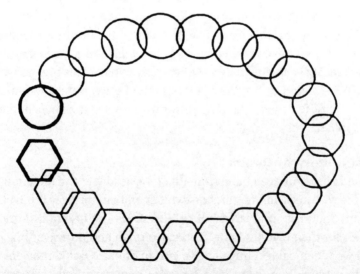

Reprinted from Bert O. States: T*he Pleasure of the Play* p71 Copyright (c) by Cornell University. Used by permission of the publisher, Cornell University Press.

For States, each circle represents a unit of dialogue and the area of overlaps indicates the cause-effect linkage of any two units. The play appears to move one step, or link, at a time in a probable direction. This direction gradually becomes elliptical, and there is a sense of convergence of all the parts as the full potential of the drama is realised. All of the events are continuous, since at no point is anything happening that is completely new. This kind of development through a series of related and overlapping episodes is also characteristic of process drama, which does not evolve through a merely linear or chronological unfolding of plot (O'Neill, 1995: 48). Instead, each episode or unit of action generates the next. The drama grows in an orbit through a chain of events that yields its full dramatic potential.

Drama does not just passively reveal, represent or reflect reality, but provides a kind of geometry for organising our perceptions. Whether in school, studio or on stage, drama is a way of thinking about life, and organising and categorising it. Many theatre artists explicitly recognise this by identifying their efforts as a laboratory. The International Theatre Research Centre is Peter Brook's title for his place of work, and he regards his dramatic experiments as arch focusing on the following questions: What is theatre? What is a play? It is an actor? What is the relationship between them all and what conditions best serve this relationship? Brook's work is a quest, and the moment something is successful it must be abandoned. It is research because it is trying to discover something, and, as Brook tells his actors, discover it through theatre so that the audience can be part of that discovery.

For Brook and other innovators, drama is a centre of psychophysical, sociological and personal experiment. Any experiment is a journey into the unknown, an entry to the labyrinth, and this quest can only be mapped after the event. Drama is always fundamentally experimental and provisional and any theory or research into drama or performance must recognise the elusive basis of the event itself. In other words, our work will always be directed 'towards a theory' and, like drama itself, in the process of becoming.

The Discourse Community

Our efforts will become true research when they are soundly based on what Madeleine Grumet (1988) identifies as 'the clarity, communication and insight of aesthetic practice' (p89). In drama, as in other fields, enquiry arises from curiosity, from wonder, from speculation about the complex nature of the enterprise and the processes by which it comes to birth, but we will also want the results of our efforts to be generative. Higher thought, theorising, is not an internalised dialogue. We claim to foster dialogue, collaboration and interpretation among our students and must not neglect these approaches in the wider research community. Genuine critical dialogue should not be replaced with contradiction, or fruitful ideas with mere irritable mental gestures. If we are to grow into scholars rather than remain students, we must always recognise and acknowledge the work of those who have gone before. It is better to be a pygmy standing on a giant's shoulders than appear to be a pygmy struggling in the dirt of dissension with other pygmies.

We must not forget that we ourselves may become influential through our teaching, writing and research. The field of drama is peopled with charismatic figures, the effect of whose personalities and ideas can be mesmerising and, at times, disabling. The tendency to reproduce ourselves spiritually among our students, co-workers and associates can be a formidable temptation. Unreflective and incompetent replication of philosophy and practice leads to a deadly inertia, while access to developing theory and effective research promotes and provokes dialogue and reflection in both students and professors.

This volume, and the institute from which it arose (Taylor, 1996), mark the beginnings of a discourse community. There is discussion, mutual appropriation and negotiated meaning. Our mission is to transform the latent energy of our research and our deliberations into educational and aesthetic substance. Ideally, this will unite us in creating, sustaining and expanding a research community. We desperately need to work in dialogue, not just in our drama but as a genuine community of scholars, researchers and practitioners. As Dewey (1927/1984) puts it, 'Ideas which are not communicated, shared, and reborn in expression are but soliloquy, and soliloquy is but broken and imperfect thought' (p371). Collaborative learning and shared discourse, which are among the distinguishing features of drama, are not merely desirable objectives but essential for the survival of our work.

True research in drama will never be a question of creating theories and cataloguing facts. It will involve growth or, more precisely, out-growth. Without abandoning its roots in practice and performance, we must find ways to show that drama can maintain itself as a discipline, integrating imagination and expression, and articulating through language and gesture the deepest concerns of our humanity. As we learn to present our theories and practice as avenues to coherence and integration in other disciplines, drama will grow outward without necessarily compromising its position as a discrete subject worthy of study. Drama has the power to enlarge our frames of reference and to emancipate us from rigid ways of thinking and perceiving. Its purpose is to bring about change – changes in practice, and changes in insight and under-standing. As Heidegger (1971) reminds us, the arts guarantee us 'a passage to those beings that we ourselves are not, and access to the being that we our-selves are' (p53).

Conclusion

To return to my metaphor of the researcher in the labyrinth, it is wise not to forget that at the dead centre of the maze lurks our research topic, the monster, its jaws dripping with the gore of scholars it has already consumed. It may pounce upon us and destroy us too, immediately or slowly. The battle may be long drawn out with neither side yielding victory. Weariness of spirit and boredom may defeat us, and we may retreat from the monster to fight another day. Or – worst scenario of all – someone may have got there before us and the monster may be already lying dead. In plain terms, the book may be already published, or the dissertation defended, or the questions answered. But there are always other labyrinths and other monsters. We will continue to be driven by what Maxine Greene (1994) has identified as an affir-mation of energy and 'the passion of reflection in a renewed hope of common action, striving for meaning, striving to understand' (p459).

Take your vorpal[1] swords in hand, and go forth, armed with pencils and note-pads, powerbooks and software. To paraphrase the words of Winston Chur-chill, we shall defend our theories and our dissertations, whatever the cost may be. We shall fight in the libraries and in the stacks, we shall fight in the footnotes and in the databases, and we shall never surrender!

Note
1 Vorpal was a word coined by Lewis Carroll to mean being 'deadly' or 'sharp'.

10

Alienation and Empowerment

Originally appeared in *Drama, Culture and Empowerment: the IDEA Dialogues*, edited by J. O'Toole and K. Donelan (1996) Brisbane: IDEA Publications. This speech was delivered at the International Drama/Theatre and Education Association in Brisbane, Australia, July, 1995.

Process drama gives access to dramatic elsewheres, imagined worlds in which students may experience new roles, novel perspectives and fresh relationships. In creating and maintaining these worlds, students construct and explore images, roles, ideas and situations. The medium of drama is available for discovering and articulating ideas, feelings and attitudes and shaping these private understandings into a public form. At its most successful, process drama displays essential empowering qualities since it is interactive, collaborative and challenging. It promotes active involvement in learning because it presents difficulties and dilemmas that may be experienced and overcome.

Instead of the teacher-generated interpretations which dominate many classrooms, process drama invites and validates the students' own responses to the unfolding dramatic event and the ideas raised within it.

In setting up a dramatic world through process drama, the teacher or leader is likely to establish some of the parameters of that world, but its articulation depends upon the conscious acceptance and collaboration of the participants. To initiate work that is truly collaborative places enormous demands on the teacher. It requires considerable flexibility, the acceptance of a degree of ambiguity, the ability to change direction and the expertise to make use of the creative responses of the group. These are all necessary qualities if the developing dramatic world is to offer genuinely empowering opportunities to students.

Too often, the worlds that are generated in drama remain teacher-directed, one-dimensional and stereotyped. They may demand little or no interrogation, elaboration or interpretation from the students. The didactic purposes of the teacher may become so obvious that the playfulness that gives life to the work is undermined. As a result, students may find themselves merely working their way through a sequence of activities stage-managed by the teacher. They may accept the role-play that is offered, but will not progress to creating roles and transcending them. The work may require little more from them than a passive agreement to take part.

Irony, a staple ingredient of dramatic worlds in the theatre, generates complex, challenging and ambiguous encounters in process drama. Its use helps teachers to avoid the obvious, the stereotyped and the didactic. In this chapter, I hope to show that when an ironic approach is used to initiate process drama, it will draw the participants into the dramatic world, challenge them to an active response and promote both judgment and interpretation. It provides a framework for investigation and permits the kind of negative reaction that, ironically, is actually constructive. Irony provides a perspective within which students may safely encounter and articulate controversial issues and ideas, discover their own values and experience the consequences of their actions.

According to the dictionary, irony consists of saying one thing and meaning the opposite. When we use irony, a message is transmitted in a manner or context that evokes a response from our audience involving a re-interpretation of our meaning. Irony is a concept that resists easy definition. We have to be alerted to its presence and understand how it operates. An acquaintance of mine was standing at the door with his four-year-old daughter, gazing at the rain. 'Another beautiful English summer day!' he said. The little girl was puzzled, so he tried to explain the concept of irony to her.

After all, he was a teacher and an academic! A little later, she took him by the hand and led him to her room. Her toys and clothes were strewn around rather artistically. 'Look, Daddy, what a tidy room!' she said with some satisfaction. She had grasped that context is all important in detecting the presence of irony. This makes it difficult to provide ironic examples out of context. Supposing that I have been behaving in a boastful and self-satisfied manner, a friend, or perhaps an enemy, may remark that I am as modest as I am beautiful. It will probably take a moment or two for the real message to reach me. In contrast, sarcasm, that blunt instrument so favoured by teachers, is self-evident and offers little challenge to reconstruction. Where sarcasm provokes resentment, irony promotes involvement. The concept of irony has been called 'vague, unstable and multiform' and more than dozen different categories have been noted.

The high points of irony in western classic drama are familiar. In *Julius Caesar*, Mark Anthony insists that Caesar's assassins are all honourable men. When he is urged to read Caesar's will by the populace he allows himself to be persuaded and his irony is unmistakable. 'I fear I wrong the honourable man whose daggers have stabbed Caesar. I do fear it.' Lady Macbeth welcomes Duncan to her home where she plans to kill him – 'He that is coming must be provided for'. When Iago warns Othello, 'Oh beware my lord of jealousy, the green eyed monster', while destroying Othello's belief in Desdemona's innocence, we, the spectators, enjoy the sense of recognition as we perceive the real meaning beneath the surface of these words and actions.

Without doubt, irony is one of the most powerful ways of setting in motion the vital, tension-producing mechanism of dramatic action and it plays as significant a role in comedy as it does in tragedy. The Irish peasants in *The Playboy of the Western World* rejoice that Pegeen will be safe this night with a man who killed his father keeping danger from her door. Lady Bracknell in *The Importance of Being Earnest*, interrogating her daughter's fiancé about his origins, responds to his acknowledgement that he has lost both parents – 'To lose one parent may be regarded as misfortune. To lose both looks like carelessness.' This play is a kind of ascending scale of ironies.

Irony is never merely a verbal matter in drama, it is also structural. Since Oedipus first called down a terrible curse upon his own head, irony has been a real comer-stone of dramatic effect, leading us to develop expectations that are certain to be reversed. Oedipus says, 'It is my solemn prayer if, with my knowledge, house or heart of mine receive the guilty man, upon my head lay all the curses I have laid on others'. The rest of the play involves the working out of these curses. In ironic drama we can be certain that, whenever any solemn promises have been made, vows pledged, curses uttered, we will see them carried out in the worst way possible or await their return on the heads of those that swore them. The most extreme reversals of fortune await the characters in drama.

Some commentators go so far as to say that all drama is essentially an ironic genre because it is concerned with impersonation and representation, but not everything that is other than it seems is an instance of irony. Nor is every time one says one thing and means another. In irony, the relationship between appearance and reality reveals itself as a contrast, an opposition, a

143

paradox and incongruity, a contradiction. It activates an endless series of subversive interpretations. It is a technique of saying as little and meaning as much as possible. It avoids direct statement and employs an objective, dispassionate attitude that allows powerful and controversial issues to be investigated and illuminated.

I first came to realise that irony was an invaluable element in structuring process drama as I began to reflect on the patterns in my own teaching and that of others, including the teaching of many of those people here in the audience. It struck me that, when a drama session went well, one of the factors in its effectiveness seemed to be the kind of ironic trap in which the participants were caught. In setting up a situation that was almost bound to provoke a negative response from students, I began to understand that, as they opposed the constraint of the situation, they were in fact accepting the drama. For example, enrolled as the Minister for Education with a class of fourteen-year-olds enrolled as eminent educators, I announce that, 'in future all sixteen- to eighteen-year-olds would receive their schooling at special institutions, isolated from their families and unable to return home for several years'. I presented this development in the most advantageous light – after all, the plan would remove students from the temptations of the street and other distractions and would give them a thorough moral and physical training. After all, it is a practice that privileged children have enjoyed for years at élite boarding schools and paid dearly for the privilege. Enrolled as educators, the students had accepted the situation but, as fourteen-year-olds, they naturally resisted it with every fibre of their being and the drama consisted of them working out that resistance.

British drama education pioneer Dorothy Heathcote, has described the irresistible mechanism that drives this kind of response. The crudest part to give others, she claims, is that of disagreeing with the role, spotting the weakness in the role's position or even opposing it. Opposition to a role places the class in a very safe position from which to disagree and oppose the teacher's power. However, the kind of resistance that is provoked in this approach may not necessarily be a crude one. The first time I worked with Heathcote, she trapped the group in a kind of absurd context which prevented us immutably from expressing our resistance. We discovered, to our surprise, that we were all people who had agreed to have our feet removed and we were naturally expected to be delighted at this turn of events. Under her guidance, we explored all the positive implications of the state of affairs and any negative aspects were held at bay as we celebrated our footless condition. Heathcote's expressed purpose was to loosen our grip on adult logic and help us to except and explore seemingly bizarre or absurd ideas.

This acceptance is saying yes to a situation without knowing where it might lead. Is it the heart of every drama event as well as being essential to the growth of improvisation? Irony provides us with an unlimited capacity to negate or oppose ideas and it is this feature that makes it invaluable for both the playwright and the drama teacher. It allows one to set up structures for debate within the parameters of a topic or theme and gives us a way of asking questions rather than supplying answers. It is a technique for dealing with concept and methodology and a complex means of presenting ideas for investigation and opposition.

One of the most sustained and devastatingly ironic texts, Jonathan Swift's *A Modest Proposal*, is in fact not a dramatic text, yet in almost every sense it is an impersonation in which Swift becomes what he opposes. In this cool, carefully argued and logical proposal, he offers a remedy for the evils of poverty and overpopulation among Irish Catholics, who lived worse than the cattle of their absentee English landlords – that these landlords should buy and eat the babies of the destitute. If this economic strategy were in place, he argues, children would no longer be a burden to their parents but a source of profit. They would be bred, raised, housed and fed at least as carefully as other domestic animals and related industries would give employment such as tanning their skins and the manufacture of delicate gloves for ladies. As he warms to the beauty and utility of his scheme, he even recommends cooking methods. Swift's savage indignation at the social ills of eighteenth century Ireland is temporarily transformed into its opposite, a smug complacency which allows him to expose those evils in pretending to address them. The cool detachment of his tone provides the horror of the piece and creates the emotional impact on the reader.

It is not too difficult to detect irony in a piece that proposes cannibalism but, in some works, there may be no obvious signpost to indicate its presence, and all the work of interpretation is left to us as we try to infer the real meaning of the message from what is said, the way it is said, who is saying it or the context. Quintilian (in Murphy, 1987) claims that irony may be made evident by the manner of delivery, the character of the speaker or the nature of the subject. An ironic attitude demands that the writer or speaker is, at least to some degree, in role and this is certainly true in process drama. Our signing can indicate that we may not mean exactly what we say. The roles we choose to play may invite interpretation, reappraisal and rejection, or the nature of the subject itself may declare that our stance must be an ironic one. If this doesn't happen and if one's intentions have not been understood as ironic, you may be denounced for holding the very opposite views to those intended.

There will never be entire agreement on when irony is at work and this ambiguity enhances a sense of productive unease, an eagerness to read the situation more closely. The 'Starship' lesson in my book *Drama Structures* is a good example of this difficulty of presentation. A male teacher enrolled as the alien who refuses to believe that males could be the officers of a spaceship might have to sign very carefully in the drama if he is to establish an ironic context for the exploration of the effects of gender discrimination.

In process drama, the most useful kind of irony is likely to be that of situation, where hidden agendas operate, purposes are disguised and expectations reversed. The more economically we can set up an ironic context for opposition and reconstruction, the more effective it will be. The aim is to achieve maximum plausibility for surface meaning and maximum conviction for the roles we play in establishing the context, while using the fewest signals we can in indicating our real meaning. Once we become explicit, irony vanishes.

As soon as an ironic voice has been identified by participants in a drama, they begin to take pleasure in the task it assigns and the qualities it promotes. The ironic voice, the impersonation which is so easily provided by the teacher-in-role becomes a highly significant part of the controlling context.

In a lesson taught by Brian Edmiston, *Space Traders*, the dramatic role that he set up was one where the remedy proposed for social ills was to ship all the unemployed and undesirable elements of society to another planet in return for financial gain – a remedy that would have acquired an extra level of irony had it taken place during an Australian history lesson. The satisfaction for the participants came in recognising, debating and resisting the demands of this dramatic world from inside that world.

The first response to the recognition of irony, the realisation that things are not what they seem, is a resounding no. There is a negative shock of recognition and, curiously enough, our unbelief is invited but, as we refuse to accept what is offered in the ironic world, we begin to accept and believe in the drama. This modified acceptance demands an alertness, a distance, a kind of alienation followed by the search for alternative interpretations, new meanings and fresh solutions.

The drama, as Milan Kundera (1986: 23) puts it in another context, is an investigation of the trap that the world has become. An ironic stance unsettles us, not because it mocks or attacks, but because it denies our certainties in exposing the world as an ambiguity. The dramatic world that is ironic is uncovered for contemplation, investigation, judgment and transformation.

I still vividly recall an in-service drama session in which a group of citizens was forced for the good of the state to build a wall to encircle the city – a difficult task that would support our future security, we were told. After much labour, our defences were complete, then we learned that the policies had changed, the wall was no longer necessary and the directive came from our leaders that we were to demolish it. Since it was in the interest of the State, we obeyed. Immediately the demolition was complete, we were once again ordered to rebuild the wall. Although it was almost twenty years ago, I have not forgotten the intense shock of alienation and recognition, an impact that was both intellectual and emotional, that was provoked by this allegory. No explication or commentary from the leader, Geoff Gillham, was necessary. As Brecht (1966: 86) put it, 'The social laws under which we were acting sprang into sight'.

The playwright or drama teacher working from an ironic perspective does not need to try to solve the mysteries of the ironic world or to cure it in any way. That is the task of the participants or the audience – those who read ironies and interpret the ambiguities. It is a key part of the method that irony must remain implicit during the event. Where it is ironic intention that is implicit, it is left to the participants to fill in the gaps, complete the hints and trace the hidden analogies. This entices the participants into acceptance and mental collaboration. There is a riddle that must be solved. The participants in the search for solutions repeat the process of invention and become co-creators of the work. As active engagement and interpretation are generated, we become kindred spirits caught in a web of collusion and this amiable community wrestles with the tasks of identification, discrimination and recognition that are necessary if the ironic conspiracy at the heart of the drama is to be disclosed.

Irony operates at a number of levels in drama. It can work as an ironic affect – as a device that works within the affective domain and the audience's emotions – within the whole structure of the play and as a dramatic structure that is itself ironic. Every smaller irony is a symptom of a larger one. In the greatest plays, it operates at every level – that of structure as well as individual utterance – and is reflected in all the imagery, symbols and character traits displayed.

The plays of Brecht are illustrations of this complexity of operation and his alienation effect can be seen as an extreme form of ironic distancing. His characters turn their backs on the implications of their actions and, instead, the audience comes to a realisation of the fundamental ironies of the play in the form of a continuous contradiction. The ironies of *Mother Courage* begin with the title and are evident in every other aspect of the play. 'Don't tell me peace has broken out when I have just gone and bought all these supplies'.

Irony in process drama works by taking a familiar social or contextual frame or scenario and displaying a variation or distortion of customary behaviour or attitude. Paradoxically, the violation of the norm is displayed but suppressed. It is never made explicit. For example, arranged marriages, computer dating and government databases are already in existence. So, in a drama about a government program where all marriages are arranged and partners are selected by computer, the dramatic structure is in itself ironic. The violated norm, the value of romantic attachments and individual choice, is suppressed. The irony consists in asserting the opposite of what is taken for granted socially. The tacit assumptions hidden in the rules of the game are dragged into the open and the associated shock shatters the frame of complacent habits of thinking. Both allegory and irony work by projecting unacceptable customs and institutions onto a different background.

In process drama, this often involves a visit to outer space or the future. The alien as a naive observer sees our creeds, customs and conventions in a new light. A few years ago, in a drama in Britain when Mrs. Thatcher was Prime Minister, a group of ten-year-olds encountered an alien from a matriarchal society who was keen to learn about political institutions in Britain. The children proudly told her that their Prime Minister was a woman. 'Naturally,' she replied, 'but have you ever had a male Prime Minister?'

The aim of using an ironic perspective is to defeat opponents on their own ground by apparently accepting their premises, values and modes of reasoning in order to expose an implicit absurdity. Irony purports to take seriously what it does not and it enters into the spirit of the opponent's game to demonstrate that the rules are stupid or vicious. It is a subtle weapon because those using it must have the imaginative power of seeing through the eyes of their opponents and of projecting themselves into the opponents' mental world. This impersonation requires a kind of understanding and empathy. The first advantage of using it in process drama is to generate the dramatic encounters that will provoke an active response. We begin to follow the trail of a complex logic and it is this pursuit that makes irony a high road to interpretation.

The ironic world created in either theatre plays or in process drama is permanently out of joint. The methods involve the selection and distortion of particular characteristics and, in selecting features for distortion like the cartoonist, one is likely to choose negative features. This affords another advantage for the drama teacher because the need for exaggeration and simplification removes the constraints of naturalism. It exposes the formal quality of the work and allows experiment with the surreal, the absurd, allegory, parody and other stylistic possibilities.

In the words of one of the Russian Formalists, irony destroys the illusion of authenticity and makes palpable the conventionality of art. The fact that the ironic world is likely to be absurdly surrealistic will not limit its effectiveness in any way. As Vygotsky (1933) points out, 'By becoming adept at creating such worlds, we use our intellect in order to become more effectively masters of the laws governing the real world'. Reality is forged from the establishment and destruction of contradictions. In process drama we can observe through the use of an ironic approach the establishment and destruction of contradictions.

If we choose an ironic pretext to launch a process drama, we will be promoting an active response in the participants and requiring them to decode the hidden agenda in the situation, to develop an opposing position and to discover their own solutions. They will move from rejection and alienation towards interpretation. One of the great advantages for the drama teacher is that by adopting this approach, basing the work on a kind of generative contradiction, the work will immediately move beyond the limits of instrumental role play. Any direct didactic quality will be obscured by the ambiguity of the approach.

Freire has emphasised the need in any kind of liberation education for these generative contradictions, balanced between the explicit and the enigmatic. Too explicit an approach may degenerate into mere propaganda with no real decoding to be done, beyond stating the obviously predetermined content. Too enigmatic, and the drama runs the risk of appearing merely to be a puzzle or a guessing game. An ironic perspective that holds a balance between the explicit and the implied will distort and subvert the kind of worthy but limited social role-plays that are frequently mistaken for drama.

We discover the absurdity of the familiar and the familiarity of the absurd. We are not fully at home in process drama until we can employ irony spontaneously to its full potential – to achieve distance, to point up absurdities, to challenge accepted norms, to defamiliarise our restrictive and oppressive social and political routines, to draw the group into community and to energise and involve the participants in a quest for effective solutions.

Epilogue

The cover image of this book is from Bertolt Brecht's *The Caucasian Chalk Circle*, a play which examines the uncompromising convictions of Grusha, a conflicted peasant woman, who kidnaps baby Michael, and embarks upon a gruelling journey over the mountains as she escapes the looming predators, the Ironshirts. The jacket photo reveals the moment when Grusha is finally captured, returns to the court, and the judge Azdak makes a test of who has rightful ownership of the child. Brecht incorporates numerous alienating techniques – music, projections, masks and puppets, multiple non-linear narratives, stylized action and incomplete characterisation. Each one activates the spectators' engagement with the play. Grusha is by no means a saintly character. Her values in taking the child, and her need to raise Michael herself, are worth scrutinising for the moral systems they reveal. One might equally say that this scrutiny and desire to interrogate are at the heart of the process drama encounter, and that Brecht's commitment to an empowering aesthetic education is no different from O'Neill's.

Brecht was a master at presenting events in less than straightforward ways and perhaps his own ambivalence toward his characters is responsible for the open-ended nature of his dramaturgy. In his play *Galileo*, for instance, the protagonist's sins of the flesh, and how these led to a recantation, appear completely human and understandable, despite the adverse implications these actions had on the evolution of science. No doubt, Brecht was a contradictory figure, and his theatrical sensibility is not for everyone, but he was profoundly experimental and he did have an ever-evolving artistic vision to which he was committed, as flawed and controversial as some might claim it was.

It might seem odd to open the Epilogue with this critique and, especially, to have a Brecht play as the jacket photo. However, as readers will have noted in *Structure and Spontaneity,* it is to the teacher's knowledge of dramatic form where we must look for directions in process drama, and educators are going to have their own specific orientations and perceptions of the work. It is informative that Ackroyd's (2004) research on teacher-in-role reveals different structural approaches that leaders have adopted in process drama. This confirms there is no one way teachers can function, but there is a general commitment to creating fictional worlds where experiences are generated for the participants' benefit and not for an external audience. There is a privileging of episodic sequencing and a desire to find distancing strategies which enable participants to understand aspects of the world in which they live. There is, most of all, a love for the artform and the requirement that educators respect their craft.

We embody what and how we teach; the medium is the message. In O'Neill's praxis, we have analysed her recurring themes and how she animates them: creating imaginary worlds, encountering dilemmas, experiencing the unexpected, shattering familiar perspectives, building belief in the situation and not the character, working from powerful pre-texts, tolerating ambiguity, implicating participants in evocative worlds and empowering the group to co-create. She was fortunate to have studied with the pre-eminent leader, Gavin Bolton, and was able to observe Dorothy Heathcote teach in numerous settings. While in recent times there has been a revisionist history written on Heathcote and Bolton, and those who commit to negotiated and collaborative process, it is important in any discipline to welcome fruitful debate and dialogue. It is somewhat ironic that the pioneering convictions of the Inner London Education Authority's Drama and Tape Centre are rarely seen in England today.

It is important that educators get in touch with their own inner rhythms and understand their thresholds for learning. Teachers need to reflect constantly on what makes for good process drama. Our teaching lives are constructed of multiple narratives. We each have our own value laden-ness. Our cultural and familial contexts, our physiology and psychology, our religious and political persuasions, our sexual, intellectual and emotional appetites all shape the kind of leaders we become as we select and implement material, and as we interact with our students and colleagues. These narrative lines can often compete with each other; they are forever evolving and sometimes in conflict.

For instance, Dorothy Heathcote has been described as 'complex, diverse, practical, poetic, inspirational and demanding' (Johnson and O'Neill, 1984: p11). Watching Heathcote teach can generate multiple observer responses, from the awestruck to the cynical. For those with a strong sense of the presentational aspect in drama, with an interest more in theatre production and performance, it can be frustrating to observe Heathcote's painstaking commitment to detail and her focus on heightening the reflective frame of participants.

Likewise, O'Neill and other proponents of process drama have been criticised for evangelising the work and for reinforcing patriarchal and universal themes, what some describe as heteronormative assumptions (see Taylor, 2006a). Recent studies in critical theory would have us deconstruct the values that are informing any particular teaching-learning encounter. How one views the world and the various theoretical lenses (such as feminism, race, Marxism, queer theory, anti-colonialism) can privilege the material that is selected and how the teacher embodies it.

Although it has not been the focus of this book to critique process drama praxis, leaders need to be conscious that how they set up work may reinforce, even unintentionally, particular worldviews. O'Neill does not see herself as a political operative in the classroom, questioning dominant ideologies, but we have seen that she is committed to the power of drama to achieve a humanising curriculum where all have a place to stand. Nonetheless, a critical theorist might anticipate a more active commentary on who wields the power at any particular time and how political hierarchies in schools impact on human development (see Ackroyd, 2006 and Taylor, 2006b, for a further discussion here).

In the introduction to Dorothy Heathcote's major writings, O'Neill with her colleague Liz Johnson (1984) describe Heathcote's lifelong concern to change the nature of schools and schooling so that there are more democratic encounters and fewer monologic edicts. That anthology, now out of print, makes an important contribution to the field as it brought Heathcote's diverse writings together and helped make accessible what appeared to be dense and sophisticated teaching. Heathcote demanded that teachers monitor whether they actually like being with children, and urged educators to detect the early warning signs of lethargy and apathy as indications that it might be time for them to move on. More significant, though, was Heathcote's challenge for leaders to plan thoroughly and to understand theatreform:

> This will include a deep understanding of the basic elements which drama and theatre share, a grasp of how time, tension, sign and symbol operate in drama, an ability to find focus, to distort productively, and to negotiate with honesty and subtlety. She urges teachers to have the courage to come to terms with themselves and to rely on what they are in their struggle for authenticity. (p13)

We see similar thematic impulses in O'Neill, whose passion and knowledge about theatre are forever present in her teaching. There is no doubt that O'Neill is a charismatic teacher; her Irish charm and humour are two key elements here, but she has made the work her own and has found clear ways of articulating complex pedagogy. Importantly, she recognises the field's pioneers and the shoulders on which she stands. She serves as a fine role model to others in that she builds a future in the immediate present, a future that is driven by past happenings and by all those magnificent teachers who have strived to secure the place of process drama in the curriculum.

When we began to put this text together, we wondered whether to include photographs of O'Neill and biographical sketches of her and her husband Colm, their three children, Rachel, Hugh and Dan, and grandchildren. While we weren't exactly rebuked for this idea, we were certainly told that this was not the way to proceed. 'This book is not about me,' she exclaimed, 'it is about the work, structure and spontaneity.' In a competitive educational climate which often promotes personality over praxis, ego over egalitarianism, it is rare and refreshing to find an outstanding educator solely concerned with the discipline.

Structure and Spontaneity: the Process Drama of Cecily O'Neill opened with the question of how educators can begin to think about designing, implementing and evaluating a drama session with integrity and which conforms to dramatic conventions and styles. Perhaps we have left you with more questions than answers but, in examining the praxis of one exceptional teacher, we hope we have provided a rich context for your own ever-evolving contemplations and teaching.

THE CECILY O'NEILL ARCHIVE

Cecily O'Neill's papers are held in an archive in the Child Drama Collection at Arizona State University. http://www.asu.edu/lib/speccoll/drama/

BOOKS
Kao, S. and C. O'Neill. (1998) *Words into Worlds: Learning a Second Language through Process Drama*. Norwood, NJ: Ablex Publishing Co.

Manley, A. and C. O'Neill. (1997) *Dreamseekers: Creative Approaches to the African American Heritage*. Portsmouth, NH: Heinemann.

O'Neill, C. (1995) *Drama Worlds: A Framework for Process Drama*. Portsmouth, NH: Heinemann.

Johnson, L. and C. O'Neill. (1984) *Dorothy Heathcote: Collected Writing on Education and Drama*. Evanston, Ill: Northwestern University Press.

O'Neill, C. and A. Lambert. (1982) *Drama Structures*, London: Hutchinson. (Translated into Danish as Dramaforlob by A. Kolstrup and C. Jantzen, 1988).

O'Neill, C. and A. Lambert, R. Linnell and J. Warr-Wood. (1976) *Drama Guidelines*. London: Heinemann.

CHILDREN'S FICTON
O'Neill, C. (1991) *Miss MacDonald had a Zoo*. London: Longman. Broadcast in the BBC program 'Listening and Reading'.

O'Neill, C. (1986) *Tim and the Wolf*. London: BBC Publications. Broadcast in the program 'Reading Corner'.

O'Neill, C. and Lambert, A. (1982) 'Allegiance and Betrayal.' In Garrett, D. (ed)(1984) *Drama Workshop Plays*. London: Macmillan.

ADAPTATIONS
O'Neill, C. (2004) The Golden Apple (unpublished) Adapted from the play by Lady Gregory.

O'Neill, C. (1987) *Sarah Plain and Tall*. Adapted for radio from the novel by Patricia MacLachlan in the children's literature series, 'Pictures in Your Mind', BBC.

ARTICLES AND PAPERS
O'Neill, C. (2004) 'The Teaching Artist.' London: London Education Arts Partnership, (LEAP), www.leaparts.info

O'Neill, C. (2003) 'Future Tense.' *Artery*, The Magazine of the Southwark Arts Forum (39), pp. 10-11.

O'Neill, C. and Murphy, S. (2002) *Interactions: The National Theatre's Education Initiative, 1998-2000.* Dublin: The National Theatre.

O'Neill, C. and Rogers, T. (2000) 'Interpretation and Resistance in Drama Worlds.' *Drama Matters,* The Journal of the Ohio Drama Education Exchange, (4), pp 21-41.

O'Neill, C. (1999a). 'The Drama Profile.' *Drama:* The Journal of National Drama, Summer, 1999.

O'Neill, C. (1999b) 'Wings Opening in the Mind.' *Theatre First,* (3), Spring.

O'Neill, C. (1999c). 'Creating Drama Worlds: Part 2.' *Youth Drama Ireland,* 1, pp 22-24.

O'Neill, C. (1999d) Foreword, *Dorothy Heathcote: Drama as a Learning Medium* by B. J. Wagner. Portsmouth: Heinemann.

O'Neill, C. (1997) 'Growing towards Democracy.' In C. Tiller (ed) *Branching Out: Drama in Eastern Europe.* London: Royal National Theatre Publications.

O'Neill, C. (1996a) 'Alienation and Empowerment.' In J. O'Toole and Donelan, K. (eds) *Drama, Culture and Empowerment: the IDEA Dialogues.* Brisbane: Idea Publications

O'Neill, C. (1996b) 'Into the Labyrinth: Research in Drama in Education.' In P. Taylor, (ed.) *Researching Drama and Arts Education: Paradigms and Possibilities.* Lewes, Sussex: Falmer Press.

O'Neill, C. (1995a) 'From Pre-text to Process: Generating Dramatic Action.' In N. McCaslin, (ed) *Children and Drama* 2nd Edition, Studio City, CA: Players Press.

O'Neill, C. (1995b) Foreword in *Drama for Learning: Dorothy Heathcote's mantle of the expert approach to learning by Heathcote,* D. and G. Bolton. Portsmouth, NH: Heinemann.

O'Neill, C., Rogers, T. and J. Jasinski. (1995). 'Transforming Texts: Intelligences in Action.' *English Journal,* 84 (Dec). pp 41-45.

O'Neill, C. (1994a) 'Walking Backwards to the Future: Teachers as Guides to New Worlds'. In B. Warren (ed) *Creating a Theatre in your Classroom.* Montreal: Captus Press.

O'Neill, C. (1994b) 'Talk and Action: Elements of the Drama Curriculum.' In J. Saxton and C. Miller, (eds) *Canadian Tertiary Drama Education: Perspectives on Practice,* Victoria, BC: University of Victoria, pp. 12-22.

O'Neill, C. (1994c). 'Here Comes Everybody: Aspects of Role in Process Drama.' *NADIE Journal,* 18, pp. 37-44.

O'Neill, C. and Rogers, T. (1994). 'Prying Open the Text.' *English in Australia,* 108, pp 47-52.

O'Neill, C. (1993) 'From Words to Worlds: Language Learning through Process Drama.' In J. Alatis (ed) *GURT 1993: Strategic Interaction and Language Acquisition: Theory, Practice and Research.* Washington, DC: Georgetown University Press

O'Neill, C. (1993) 'Drama in Education.' In A. Purves (ed) *Encyclopedia of English Studies and Language Arts.* New York: Scholastic.

O'Neill, C. (1992) 'Drama in the Classroom: The Search for Dramatic Action.' In J. Hughes (ed) *Drama Teaching: The State of the Art,* Sydney: The Australian Association for the Teaching of English.

O'Neill, C. and T. Rogers (1992) 'Creating Multiple Worlds: Drama and Literary Response.' In G. Newell and R.K. Durst (eds) *Exploring Texts: The Role of Discussion and Writing in the Teaching and Learning of Literature.* Norwood, MA: Christopher-Gordon.

O'Neill, C. (1991a) 'Dramatic Worlds: Structuring for Significant Experience', *The Drama Theatre Teacher,* 4 (1), pp. 3-5.

O'Neill, C. (1991b) 'Artists and Models: Theatre Teachers for the Future', *Design for Arts in Education,* 92 (4), pp. 23-27.

O'Neill, C. (1991c). 'Training Teachers.' *Teaching Theatre*, 2(4), pp. 1-2, 5-6.

O'Neill, C. (1989a) 'Contexts, Roles and Evaluation.' In J. Kase-Polisini (ed) *Drama as a Meaning Maker*. Lanham, MD: University Press of America.

O'Neill, C. (1989b). 'Dialogue and Drama: transformation of events, ideas, and teachers.' *Language Arts*, 66 (2), pp. 147-59.

O'Neill, C. (1988a) 'Ways of Seeing: Audience Function in Drama and Theatre,' *NADIE Journal* 13, pp. 11-17.

O'Neill, C. (1988b) 'The Nature of Dramatic Action,' *NADIE Journal* 12, pp. 2-7.

O'Neill, C (1988c) 'Exploring a Topic through Role-Play and Drama,' *Voices*, Journal of the English Language Arts Council of the Alberta Teacher's Association, 3, pp. 6-9.

O'Neill, C. (1988d) 'The Wild Things go to School', *Drama Contact*, The Council of Drama in Education, Ontario, 12, pp. 3-6.

O'Neill, C. (1986) 'Beruhmte Leute', *Praxis Deutsch*, 76, pp. 56-59.

O'Neill, C. (1985). 'Imagined Worlds in theatre and drama', *Theory into Practice*, 24 (Summer), pp. 158-65.

O'Neill, C. (1983a). 'Context or Essence.' In Day, C. and Norman, J. (eds) *Issues in Educational Drama*. London and New York: Falmer Press.

O'Neill, C. (1983b) 'Role-play and Text', *The English Magazine*, 11, pp. 19-21.

O'Neill, C. (1981a) 'Freedom through Work', *London Drama Magazine*, 6 (5), pp. 10-12.

O'Neill, C. (1981b) 'Beast Behaviour: Classroom drama and Role-play', *Child Education*, November, 21.

O'Neill, C. (1981c) 'Drama with Everything: Enriching the Curriculum', *Junior Education*, March, 3

O'Neill, C. (1980a) 'Drama in Education – Active Experience', *Nordisk Drama-pedagogisk*, 4.

O'Neill, C. (1980b) 'Jesu fodsel sett pa ny', *Nordisk Drama-pedagogisk*, Julen 4, pp. 16-20.

O'Neill, C. (1980c) 'Arts and Education', *ABRACADABRA*, The Association of British Columbia Drama Educators, 2 (2), pp. 4-8.

O'Neill, C. (1979a) 'Justifying the Place of Drama in Education', *CCYDA Journal* (Canadian Child and Youth Drama Association, Winter, pp. 15-21.

O'Neill, C. (1979b) 'Time, Structure and Experience', *NADECT Journal* (National Association for Drama in Education and Children's Theatre), 13, pp. 24-28

O'Neill, C. (1979c) 'Re-live the Nativity', *Junior Education*, November, pp.16-18

O'Neill C. and Lambert, A. (1979) 'Co-artists in the Creative Drama Process', *CCYDA Journal* (Canadian Child and Youth Drama Association, Spring, pp. 8-13

CURRICULUM AND BROADCAST MATERIALS

O'Neill, C. (2001) *The Archives Resource Box: An introduction to the History of the Abbey Theatre*. Dublin: Abbey Theatre

O'Neill, C. Series Editor for the series 'Plays Plus', 'Short Plays Plus, 'Classics Plus' and 'Upstagers', London: Collins Educational, London. There are more than twenty titles in the series, which is accompanied by resource materials

O'Neill, C. Consultant Editor for 'Macmillan Drama Anthologies' published by Macmillan Education, London

O'Neill, C. Author of a number of radio scripts for the BBC programmes 'Drama Workshop', 'Junior Drama Workshop' and 'First Steps in Drama'

RESEARCH

O'Neill, C. (2005a) *Imagination in Action: Unicorn Education 1997-2005*. An evaluative report on the Unicorn's Education Programme

O'Neill, C. (2005b) *Artformations*. Evaluative Report on a joint project between Ireland's National Theatre and the Irish Museum of Modern Art. Funded by the Arts Council of Ireland

O'Neill, C. (2003a) *Stepping Out*. Evaluative Report on 'EziMotion', a pilot project by CoisCeim Dance Theatre, funded by the Arts Council of Ireland

O'Neill, C. (2003b) *Future Tense*. A practical research and development project in a London school with the Unicorn Theatre

O'Neill, C. (2002). Evaluative Report on the Unicorn Theatre's *Great Expectation* Residency, funded by the London Arts Partnership

O'Neill, C. (2001). Evaluative Report on the Unicorn Theatre's *Red Red Shoes Education Project*, funded by the London Arts Board and the Place Theatre

O'Neill, C. (1998-2000). *Abbey Encounters*. An investigation and evaluation of 'Inter-actions', the Irish National Theatre's Education Initiative. Funded by the Department of Education and Science, the Gulbenkian Foundation and the Arts Council

O'Neill, C. (1998-99). *Education and Research Initiative*, funded by the Arts Council of England. An investigation of the integration of the Unicorn Theatre's education pro-gramme into the heart of the organization

PROFESSIONAL RECOGNITION

Appointed *Associate Artist* at the Unicorn Children's Theatre, London, 2001

Member of the Advisory Forum for Outreach/Education at the Abbey Theatre, 2000

The Cecily O'Neill Teacher Education Research Award was established in Dr. O'Neill's name at IDIERI 2000, the International Drama in Education Research Institute, held at The Ohio State University in July 2000.

Medallion Recipient from the Children's Theater Foundation of America for Significant Achievement and Contribution to Theatre for Children and Youth in the United States, July 1999

The Annual Distinguished Book Award from AATE, The American Alliance for Theatre and Education, 1998, for 'Dreamseekers: Creative Approaches to the African American Heri-tage.' By Manley, A. and C. O'Neill, 1998 (Portsmouth, NH: Heinemann)

The Annual Science Research Award from the National Science Council of Taiwan for 'Teaching and Learning a Second Language through Drama Activities: Theory and Practice.' by Kao, S. and C. O'Neill, 1996-1998

Elected to the position of *Honorary Visiting Professor* at The University of Central England, Birmingham, 1998

Lifetime Achievement Award, The Ohio Drama Education Exchange, July 1998

Patron, London Drama, (Drama Teacher's Professional Association)

Patron, Graffiti Theatre in Education Company, Cork, Ireland

VIDEO AND AUDIO MATERIALS

Work featured in TV and radio programs includes:

February 2001. Drama workshop filmed by the National Television Company of Finland

January, 2001. Radio interview for Radio Telefis Eireann programme, 'Rattlebag'

October 1999. Radio interview for Radio Telefis Eireann

July, 1995. Interview for 'Statewide', a program produced by The Queensland Performing Arts Trust for TV Education, broadcast by SBS

October, 1994. A series of TV interviews for the Media and Broadcasting Unit of the Maltese Department of Education, October, 1994 for inclusion in 'A Mirror of Life', a series of educational programs devoted to the appreciation of literature and filmed in the National Library of Malta in Valletta

1991. Featured on the teaching video 'Innovative Strategies in the French Immersion Classroom', Part 11, *Language in Action*, funded by the US Department of Education.

1991. Subject of a TV program, *Innovators in Education*, produced by T.V. Ontario

1990. Featured on a training video for teachers produced by the London and East Anglican Examinations Board

References

Ackroyd, J. (ed) (2006) *Research Methodologies for Drama Education*. Stoke on Trent: Trentham.

Ackroyd, J. (2004) *Role Reconsidered: A re-evaluation of the relationship between teacher-in-role and acting*. Stoke on Trent: Trentham.

Anderson, P. (1994) 'Four facts everyone ought to know about science', *Daily Telegraph*, 31 August.

Beckerman, B. (1972) 'What the Silence Said: Still points in King Lear.' In Leech and Margeson (eds) *Shakespeare 1971; Proceedings of the World Shakespeare Congress,* Vancouver, August 1971. Toronto: University of Toronto Press.

Beckerman, B. (1970) *Dynamics of Drama*. New York: Alfred Knopf.

Benton, M. (1992) *Secondary Worlds: Literature Teaching and the Visual Arts*. Philadelphia, PA: Open University Press.

Berlyne, D.E. (1960) *Conflict, Arousal and Curiosity*. New York: McGraw-Hill.

Bolton, G. (2003) *Dorothy Heathcote: biography of remarkable drama teacher*. Stoke on Trent: Trentham.

Bolton, G. (1984) *Drama as Education: An argument for placing drama at the centre of the curriculum*. London: Longman.

Bolton, G. (1979) *Towards a theory of drama in education*. London: Longman.

Bolton, G. (1978) 'Emotion in the dramatic process – is it an adjective or a verb?' *NADIE Journal*. Vol. 3, pp 14-18.

Bolton, G. (1977) 'Creative Drama as an Art Form.' *London Drama*. 26(2), pp. 10-12.

Booth, D. (1987) *Drama Words: The role of drama in language growth*. Toronto: Language Study Centre, Toronto Board of Education.

Booth, W. (1974) *Rhetoric of Irony*. Chicago: The University of Chicago Press.

Booth, W. (1961) *The Rhetoric of Fiction*. Chicago, IL: University of Chicago Press.

Britton, J. (1970) *Language and Learning*. London: Penguin.

Brecht, B. (1966) *Brecht on Theatre*. New York: Hill and Wang.

Brook, P. (1972) *The Empty Space*. London: Penguin.

Bruner, J. (1962) *On Knowing: Essays for the Left Hand*. New York: Atheneum.

Bruner, J. (1960) *The Process of Education*. Cambridge, MA: Harvard University Press.

Burke, K. (1969) *A Grammar of Motives*. Berkeley, CA: University of California Press.

Burke, M. (1983) 'Cecily O'Neill at U.B.C.' *Abracadabra, Journal of Association of British Columbia Drama Educators*. 5(2), pp. 11-12.

Burns, E. (1978) *Theatricality: a study of convention in the theatre and in social life.* London: Longman.

Byron, K. (1986) *Drama in the English Classroom.* New York: Methuen.

Cassirer, E. (1944) *An Essay on Man.* New Haven: Yale University Press.

Child, I. L. (1969) 'Esthetics.' In Lindzey and Aronson (eds) *Handbook of Social Psychology.* 2nd Ed. Vol. III. Reading, MA: Addison-Wesley Publishing Co.

Cohen-Cruz, J. and M. Schutzman (eds) (2006) *A Boal Companion: Dialogues on theatre and cultural politics.* New York: Routledge.

Collier, G. (1975) *Jazz.* Cambridge: Cambridge University Press.

Courtney, R. (1982) *Re-Play: Studies in Human Drama and Education.* Toronto: OISE Press.

Courtney, R. (1977) 'The Discipline of Drama,' *Queen's Quarterly.* Ontario.

Courtney, R. (1971) 'Drama and Pedagogy,' *Stage-Canada Supplement.* 6 (1), p. 5a.

Courtney, R. (1968) *Play, Drama and Thought.* London: Cassell.

Davies, G. (1983) *Practical Primary Drama.* Portsmouth: Heinemann.

Davis, D (2005) *Edward Bond and the Dramatic Child; Edward Bond's plays for young people.* Stoke on Trent: Trentham.

Davis, D. and C. Lawrence (1986) *Gavin Bolton: Selected writings.* Essex: Longman.

Day, C. (1975) *Drama for Upper and Middle Schools.* London: Batsford.

Dewey, J. (1927/1984) *John Dewey: The Later Works Vol. 11.* New York: Collier.

Dewey, J. (1934) *Art as Experience.* London: Allen and Unwin.

Eco, U. (1994) *The Limits of Interpretation.* Bloomington, IN: University of Indiana Press.

Eco, U. (1987) *Travels in Hyper-Reality.* London: Pan Books.

Eco, U. (1984) *The Role of the Reader: Explorations in the semiotics of texts.* Bloomington, In: Indiana University Press.

Edmiston, B., P. Enciso, and M. L. King. (1987) 'Empowering Readers and Writers Through Drama: Narrative theatre.' *Language Arts*, 64, pp. 219-229.

Ehrenzweig, A. (1967) *The Hidden Order of Art.* London: Paladin.

Eisner, E. (1985a) *The Educational Imagination: On the Design and the Evaluation of School Programs.* New York: Macmillan.

Eisner, E. (1985b) *Learning and Teaching: The Ways of Knowing.* Chicago, IL: University of Chicago Press.

Eisner, E. (1972) *Educating Artistic Vision.* New York: Macmillan.

Ejxenbaum, B.M. (1922) 'O. Henry and the Theory of the Short Story.' In L. Matejka and K. Pomorska (eds) *Readings in Russian Poetics* (1978). Anne Arbor, MI, University of Michigan Press.

Elam, K. (1980) *The Semiotics of Theatre and Drama.* London: Methuen.

Erikson, Erik. (1963) *Childhood and Society.* New York: Norton and Co. Ltd.

Feldman, E.B., (1970) 'Engaging Art in Dialogue.' In G. Pappas (ed) *Concepts in Art and Education.* New York: Macmillan.

Fines, J. and Verrier, R. (1974) *The Drama of History.* London: Clive Bingley Ltd.

Freire, P. (1972) *Pedagogy of the Oppressed.* London: Penguin Books.

Gardner, H. (1991) *The Unschooled Mind: How Children Think and How Schools Should Teach.* New York: Basic Books.

Gardner, H. (1983) *Frames of Mind: The Theory of Multiple Intelligence.* New York: Basic Books.

Gassner, J. (1956) *Form and Idea in Modern Theatre*. New York: Holt, Rinehart and Winston.

Goffman, I. (1974) *Frame Analysis*. New York: Harper and Row.

Goleman, J. (1986) 'The Dialogic Imagination: More Than We've Been Taught.' In Thomas Newkirk (ed) *Only Connect: Uniting Reading and Writing*. New Jersey: Boynton/Cook.

Gotshalk, D.W. (1947) *Art and the Social Order*. Chicago, IL: University of Chicago.

Greene, M. (1994) Lincoln Centre Institute for the Arts In Education. New York City, Unpublished lectures, July 21.

Greene, M. (1971) *The Dialectic of Freedom*. London: Oliver and Boone.

Grumet, M. R. (1988) *Bitter Milk: Women and teaching*. Amherst: University of Massachusetts Press.

Grumet, M. R. (1978) 'Curriculum as Theatre: Merely Players.' *Curriculum Inquiry* (8), pp. 37-64.

Hardy, B. (1977) 'Towards a Poetics of Fiction: An Approach Through Narrative.' In M. Meek *et al.* (eds). The Cool Web. London: Bodley Head.

Heathcote, D. (1982) *Heathcote at the National: Drama Teacher-Facilitator or Manipulator?* T. Goode (ed). Banbury, Kemble Press.

Havell, C. (1987) 'A Reconstruction of the Development of Drama in Education.' In P. Abbs (ed) *Living Powers* Lewes, Falmer Press.

Heathcote, D. and Bolton, G. (1995) *Drama for Learning: Dorothy Heathcote's mantle of the expert approach to education*. Portsmouth, NH: Heinemann.

Heathcote, D. (1978) 'Of these seeds becoming.' In R. Shuman (ed) *Educational drama for today's schools*. Metuchen, NJ: Scarecrow Press.

Heidegger, M. (1971) *Poetry, Language, Thought* (Albert Hofstadter, Trans.). New York: Harper and Row.

Hornby, R. (1986) *Drama, Metadrama, and Perception*. Lewisburg: Bucknell University Press.

Huizinga, J. (1955) *Homo Ludens*. Boston: Beacon.

Huxley, A. (1977) *Brave New World*. London: Chatto and Windus.

Isaacs, S. (1935) *Social Development in Young Children*. London: Routledge and Kegan Paul.

Iser, W. (1978) *Act of Reading: A Theory of Aesthetic Response*. Baltimore, MD: Johns Hopkins Press.

Johnson, L. and C. O'Neill (1984) *Dorothy Heathcote: Collected Writings on Education and Drama*. Cheltenham: Stanley Thornes.

Johnstone, K. (1979) *Improv*. London: Faber and Faber.

Kant, I. (1951) *Critique of Judgement*. New York: Hafner Press.

King, N. R. (1986) 'Recontextualizing the Curriculum.' *Theory into Practice*, 25, pp. 36-40.

Koestler, A. (1975) *The Act of Creation*. London: Picador.

Kundera, M. (1986) *The Arts of the Novel*. New York: Grove Press.

Langer, S. (1957a) *Problems of Art*. London: Routledge and Kegan Paul.

Langer, S. (1957b) *Philosophy in a New Key: A study in the symbolism of reason, rite and art*. Harvard University Press: Cambridge, MA.

Langer, S. (1953) *Feeling and Form*. New York: Scribner.

Lemon, L.T., and Reis, M. J. (1965) *Russian Formalist Criticism: Four Essays*. Lincoln: University of Nebraska Press.

Manley, A. and C. O'Neill (1997) D*reamseekers: Creative Approaches to the African American Heritage*. Portsmouth, NH: Heinemann.

McGregor, L., Tate, M. and Robinson, K. (1977) *Learning through Drama: Report of the Schools Council Drama Teaching Project (10-16)*. London: Heinemann.

McLaren, P. (1988) 'The Liminal Servant and the Ritual Roots of Critical Pedagogy,' *Language Arts*, 65, pp. 164-179.

McLaren, P. (1986) *Schooling as a Ritual Performance: Towards a Political Economy of Educational Symbols and Gestures*. London: Routledge and Kegan Paul.

Mead, M. (1934) *Mind, Self, and Society*. Chicago: University of Chicago Press.

Medawar, P. (1982) *Plato's Republic*. Oxford: Oxford University Press.

Merleau-Ponty, M. (1967) *The Phenomenology of Perception*. Evanston, IL: Northwestern University Press.

Moffett, J. (1968) *Teaching the Universe of Discourse*. Boston: Houghton Mifflin.

Morgan, N., and Saxton, J. (1987) *Teaching Drama*. London: Hutchinson.

Muecke, D.C. (1970) *Irony and the Ironic*. London: Methuen.

Murphy, J. (1987) *Quintilian on the Teaching of Speaking and Writing*. Illinois: Southern Illinois University Press.

O'Neill, C. (1997) 'Aspects of the process.' In A. Manley and C. O'Neill (eds) *Dreamseekers*. Portsmouth: Heinemann, pp. 85-103.

O'Neill, C. (1995) *Drama Worlds: A framework for process drama*. Portsmouth, New Hampshire: Heinemann.

O'Neill, C. (1991) 'Artists and Models: Theatre Teachers for the Future.' *Design for Arts in Education*, 92 (4), pp. 23-27.

O'Neill, C. (1980) 'Arts and Education.' *Abracadabra: Journal of Association of British Columbia Drama Educators*, 2 (2), pp. 4-7.

O'Neill, C (1979) 'Time, Structure and Experience,' *Outlook*, 13, pp.24-28.

O'Neill, C. (1978) Drama and the Web of Form. Unpublished MA dissertation, University of Durham.

O'Neill, C. and Lambert, A. (1982) *Drama Structures: A practical handbook for teachers*. Cheltenham: Stanley Thornes.

O'Neill, C., A. Lambert, R. Linnell, and Warr-Wood, J. (1976) *Drama Guidelines*, London, Heinemann Educational Books in association with London Drama.

O'Neill, C. and Rogers, T. (1994) 'Prying Open the Text.' *English in Australia* 108, pp. 47-52.

Parsons, M.J. (1970) 'The Concept of Medium in Education.' In R. A. Smith (ed) *Aesthetic Concepts and Education*. Urbana, IL: University of Illinois Press.

Piaget, J. (1962) *Play, Dreams, and Imitation in Childhood*. New York: Norton.

Pippard, B. (1986) 'Complementary copies.' In K. Egan (ed) *Primary standing* (1991) New York: Routledge.

Polanyi, M. (1962) *Personal Knowledge*. Chicago: University of Chicago Press

Read, H. (1931) *The Meaning of Art*. London: Pelican.

Reid, L. A. (1969) *Meaning in the Arts*. London: Allen and Unwin.

Reid, L. A. (1961) *Ways of Knowledge and Experience*. London: Allen and Unwin.

Reilly, M. (1974) *Play as Exploratory Learning*. Beverly Hills, CA: Sage.

Robinson, K. (1983) A re-evaluation of the roles and functions of drama in secondary education. Unpublished doctoral dissertation, University of London, London: England.

Roethke, T. (1977) 'Dolor.' In G. Moore (ed) *The Penguin Book of America.* London: Penguin.

Rogers, T. and O'Neill, C. (1993) 'Creating Multiple Worlds: Drama, Language, and Literary Response.' In G. Newell and R. Durst (eds) *Exploring Texts*, Norwood, NJ: Christopher-Gordon.

Rosen, H. (1980) 'The Dramatic Mode.' In P. Salmon (ed) *Coming to Know.* London: Routledge and Kegan Paul.

Rosenberg, H. (1987) *Creative Drama and Imagination: Transforming Ideas into Action.* New York: Holt, Rinehart and Winston.

Rosenberg, H. (1962) *The Tradition of the New.* London: Paladin.

Santayana, G. (1958) 'George Santayana on Existentialism: An unpublished letter,' *Partisan Review,* 25:635, 637.

Santayana, G. (1955) *The Sense of Beauty.* New York: Dover.

Shor, I. and Freire, P. (1987) *A Pedagogy for Liberation: Dialogues on Transforming Education.* South Hadley, MA: Bergin and Garvey.

Singer, J.L. (1973) *The Child's World of Make-Believe.* New York: Academic Press.

Slade, P. (1954) *Child Drama.* London: University of London Press.

Smilansky, S. (1963) *The Effects of Socio-Dramatic Play on Disadvantaged Children.* New York: John Wiley.

Smith, R. A. (1970) *Aesthetic Concepts and Education.* Urbana, IL: University of Illinois Press.

Spolin, V. (1964) *Improvisation for the Theatre.* Evanston, IL: Northwestern University Press.

Spolin, V. (1963) *Theatre Games.* Evanston, IL: Northwestern University Press.

Stanislavski, C. (1936/1969) *An Actor Prepares.* London: Geoffrey Bles.

States, B.O. (1994) *The Pleasure of the Play.* Ithaca: Cornell University Press.

States, B.O. (1971) *Irony and Drama.* Ithaca, NY: Cornell University Press.

Steinberg, L. (1972) *Other Criteria.* New York: Oxford University Press.

Stephenson, J. (1985) *That Dreadful Day.* New York: Greenwillow Books.

Sterne, L. (1983) *The Life and Opinions of Tristram Shandy*, Gentleman. London: Clarendon Press.

Stewart, S. (1981) 'Shouts on the Street: Bakhtin's Antilinguistics.' In G. S. Morson (ed) *Bakhtin: Essays and Dialogues on his Work.* Chicago, IL: University of Chicago Press.

Stolnitz, J. (1960) *Aesthetics and Philosophy of Art Criticism.* New York: Houghton Mifflin Co.

Storr, A. (1972) *The Dynamics of Creation.* London: Secker and Warburg.

Swift, J. (1729/1955) *Irish Tracts.* Oxford: Blackwell.

Szondi, P. (1987) *Theory of the Modern Drama.* Minneapolis, MN: University of Minnesota Press.

Taylor, P. (2006a) 'Power and Privilege: re-envisioning the qualitative research lens.' In Ackroyd, J.(ed) *Research Methodologies for Drama Educators.* Stoke on Trent: Trentham, pp1-14.

Taylor, P. (2006b) *Assessment in Arts Education.* Portsmouth: Heinemann.

Taylor, P. (2000) *The Drama Classroom: Action, Reflection, Transformation.* London: RoutledgeFalmer.

Taylor, P. (1998) *Redcoats and Patriots: Reflective practice in drama and social studies.* Portsmouth, NH: Heinemann.

Taylor, P. (ed)(1996) *Researching Drama and Arts Education: Paradigms and Possibilities.* London: Falmer.

Turner, V. W. (1969) *The Ritual Process: Structure and Anti-Structure.* Chicago: Aldine.

Ultan, L. (1989) 'Crises in Society: The role of the arts,' *Design for Arts in Education*, 90 (5) (May/June), p.14.

Verriour, P. (1985) 'Face to Face: Negotiating Meaning through Drama,' *Theory into Practice*, 24, pp. 181-186.

Vivas, E. and Krieger, M. (1965) *The Problems of Aesthetics.* New York: Holt, Rinehart and Winston.

Vygotsky, L. (1971) *The Psychology of Art.* Cambridge, MA: MIT Press.

Vygotsky, L. (1933/1976) 'Play and its role in the mental development of the child.' In Bruner, J.S., Jolly, A. and K. Sylva (eds) *Play: Its Role in Development and Evolution.* New York: Penguin.

Wagner, B.J. (1998) *Educational Drama and Language Arts: What research shows.* Portsmouth, NH: Heinemann.

Wagner, B.J. (1988) 'Research currents: does classroom drama affect the arts of language?' *Language Arts* 65 (1).

Wagner, B.J. (1976) *Dorothy Heathcote: Drama as a Learning Medium.* London: Hutchinson.

Ward, W. (1930) *Creative Dramatics.* New York: Appleton.

Warnock, M. (1976) *Imagination.* London: Faber.

Watling, E.F. (trans.) (1947) *Oedipus Rex.* Harmondsworth, Middlesex: Penguin Books.

Way, B. (1967) *Development Through Drama.* London: Longman.

Witkin, R.W. (1974) *The Intelligence of Feeling.* London: Heinemann Education.

Wright, L. (1985) 'Preparing teachers to put drama in the classroom,' *Theory into Practice*, 24 (3).

Woodbury, L. J. (1976) *Mosaic Theatre.* Provo, Utah: Brigham Young University Press.

Yeats, W.B. (1923) 'The Only Jealousy of Emer.' In *Plays and Controversies.* London: Macmillan.

Index

167